Both Sides

of

Recovery

MELISSA & HARRY HARRISON

PAULIST PRESS
New York/Mahwah, N.J.

Acknowledgements

THE TWELVE STEPS OF ALCOHOLICS ANONYMOUS

1. We admitted we were powerless over alcohol—that our lives had become unmanageable. 2. Came to believe that a Power greater than ourselves could restore us to sanity. 3. Made a decision to turn our will and our lives over to the care of God <u>as we understood Him</u>. 4. Made a searching and fearless moral inventory of ourselves. 5. Admitted to God, to ourselves and to another human being the exact nature of our wrongs. 6. Were entirely ready to have God remove all these defects of character. 7. Humbly asked Him to remove our shortcomings. 8. Made a list of all persons we had harmed, and became willing to make amends to them all. 9. Made direct amends to such people wherever possible, except when to do so would injure them or others. 10. Continued to take personal inventory and when we were wrong promptly admitted. it. 11. Sought through prayer and meditation to improve our conscious contact with God, <u>as we understood Him</u>, praying only for knowledge of His will for us and the power to carry that out. 12. Having had a spiritual awakening as the result of these steps, we tried to carry this message to alcoholics, and to practice these principles in all our affairs.

The Twelve Steps were reprinted with permission of Alcoholics Anonymous World Services, Inc. Permission to reprint the Twleve Steps does not mean that A.A. has reviewed or approved the contents of this publication, nor that A.A. agrees with the views expressed herein. A.A. is a program of recovery from alcoholism <u>only</u>—use of the Twelve Steps in connection with other programs and activities which are patterned after A.A., but which address other problems, or in any other non-A.A. context, does not imply otherwise.

Book design by Theresa M. Sparacio

Cover design by Arthur W. Simmons

Library of Congress Cataloging-in-Publication Data

Harrison, Melissa, 1951-
    Both sides of recovery / by Melissa & Harry Harrison.
        p.   cm.
    Includes bibliographical refences.
    ISBN 0-8091-3633-3 (alk. paper)
    1. Recovering alchoholics—United States—Case studies. 2. Recovering addicts—United States—Case studies. 4. Narcotic addicts—Rehabilitation—United States—Case studies. 5. Alcoholics' spouses—United States—Case studies. 6. Twelve-step programs—United States, Case studies. I. Harrison, Harry, 1948- II. Title.
HV5279.H37   1996
362.29´2´0973—dc20   95-49268
                                                                 CIP

Published by Paulist Press
997 Macarthur Boulevard
Mahwah, NJ 07430

Printed and bound in the
United States of America

TO SUSAN AND BILL,
WHO SHOWED US THE WAY.
AND TO SAGE AND FIELD,
WHO WERE THERE WAITING.

My Name Is

MELISSA

Prologue

*T*he Twelve Steps I'm about to discuss have changed my life and have allowed me to stop using any mind-altering chemicals since 1985. That was the year my addiction to drugs practically swallowed me whole. When I refer to drugs in the following pages, I'm including alcohol, prescription pills, street drugs and over-the-counter remedies such as cough medicine and sleeping aids. In my book, anything that alters reality is a drug. I have to constantly remember that just because it comes off a physician's prescription pad doesn't make it okay. In my case, quite the opposite was true.

I began to understand this concept my first morning in the treatment center. The doctor explained to me that a person's brain cannot tell the difference between an injection of heroin or a shot of whiskey. The synapses and neurotransmitters react similarly, whether it's alcohol or drugs we're ingesting. Over the years, I've talked to hundreds of alcoholics and drug addicts, and I've arrived at the same conclusion. Most mind-altering chemicals affect the brain's chemistry in the same way. The one thing we can all agree upon is this: drugs always wreak havoc in an addict's life.

When the drug is removed, the addict is left with a painful emotional vacuum. Some addicts describe it as a hole in their gut. Psychiatrists and theologians alike define it as a yearning, both physical and spiritual. This yearning or sense of emptiness will ultimately take addicts back to their drug of choice if some relief isn't offered. I am a relief junkie. I love anything that gives me a sense of case and comfort. I've tried just about every available substance and behavior to find that relief. The Twelve Steps offered to me in my drug recovery have given me the peace of mind and coping skills that I searched for elsewhere. The steps enable me to live comfortably in this world and within my own skin without drugs.

I tried to make other people, places and things do that for me my first thirty-five years of life. But the relief that came from these external sources couldn't be sustained. Eventually the person I was using would give out; the money would run out; or the drug would simply quit working. Only by working the steps have I found a level of comfort which increases with time. Unlike drugs, the effects do not diminish over time; or in drug jargon, I don't build up a tolerance to them. There is hope for addiction. It's simple, but it is not easy. If you're an addict, your life is far from easy anyway. You don't have anything to lose by trying the steps. Early death doesn't frighten addicts, but the thought of living without drugs usually scares us to death.

STEP ONE. We admitted we were powerless over alcohol and drugs—that our lives had become unmanageable.

*T*he first time I knew I was powerless over drugs and alcohol, I was about ten years old. My parents were having a cocktail party and things got loud enough to wake me. When I stepped out of my bedroom and saw how my parents and their friends were acting, I experienced the ripple of fear that comes whenever I look into the eyes of something wild and dangerous. The next morning while my parents slept, I cleaned out ashtrays and took dirty glasses to the kitchen. If you had asked me if I felt power-less the night before I wouldn't have known what you meant. I felt angry and a little embarrassed. But mainly, I was afraid.

My mother tells me that the first time I was drunk I was five years old. We were at a wedding and I drank a couple of flutes of champagne, then proceeded to stumble and weave around the room prior to taking a very long nap. Apparently, it was an amusing spectacle for the presiding adults. I don't remember it.

I grew up in Billings, Montana during the mid-1950s and 1960s. My parents were young and rich and heavy drinkers. They fought like crazy. On more nights than I care to recall, they'd start drinking, then a battle would ensue. Dinner burned on the stove while my brothers and I gnawed on crackers and pestered mom to feed us. I never thought alcohol was the problem; I just thought my parents were crazy. I would watch "Father Knows Best" or "Leave it to Beaver" on TV and long for a normal family like the ones I saw bounce through life on the television screen.

As my parents' drinking escalated, so did their fighting. By the time I was thirteen, they divorced. I rebelled and acted out my anger by dating the town delinquent. I was promptly sent away to a girls' school in Minnesota. If this was meant to be punitive, it backfired. I grew to love the routine, the structure, the three meals a day. I actually gained weight (my severe thinness had been a constant source of concern for my mother) and started to learn how to concentrate on schoolwork. But, money ran out and I was back at home the following year attending a public high school.

Things temporarily smoothed out a little at home. My younger brothers and I got used to having our father gone. I no longer fought with my mother every day. In fact, our relationship shifted dramatically. It was as if I were her partner; she said I was her best friend. I helped her with all the housework, and took care of my brothers while mother attended college. I felt like a grown-up. So grown-up, in fact, that my schoolmates appeared terribly immature and shallow. Things like pep rallies and school proms seemed ridiculous; I was immersed in real-life responsibilities, having adult conversations, doing adult things.

On my fifteenth Christmas Eve, a widow friend of my mother's brought her daughters over for dinner. They carried in a large cardboard box containing liquor, crème de menthe and assorted other bottles of booze. We proceeded to sample every one of them. These girls, like myself, were fatherless, and they, too, had grown up fast. That was the first time I recall getting drunk. I ranted and raved at the top of the stairs, then I threw up for two hours.

After that, I drank on most weekends with one or two

girlfriends. We quickly learned that if we drank and drove, we usually crashed our cars into something, whether it was another car or a trash can; the results were always costly. So we usually stayed at one of our houses where the parents were gone, and we would drink whiskey, giggle, smoke cigarettes, then take two aspirin to ward off a headache, and go to bed. We were never caught.

My grandmother lived a few blocks from my house. She was the safety net for our family. Whenever my father would forget to send child support or an emergency came up (and with three kids, there were many emergencies), Mimi would pull out her checkbook and cover our expenses. She had a spotless house, cooked fragrant, hearty meals, and never trusted a soul who didn't drink.

Sometimes after school, I'd stop by her house where she taught me how to mix a "ditch," which was two jiggers of bourbon and water. Instead of cookies and milk with granny, my friends and I often had a ditch and a cigarette with Mimi. She'd let us drive her big Cadillac around on summer nights. I dented it in a few times, but she never scolded me and the car was as good as new when I returned for my next visit.

Mimi's house was a respite for me. There were no brothers to take care of, no responsibilities. This was a quiet and safe place where I could retreat and get a good meal and some sane advice when I asked for it. I often think I would have lost my mind if I hadn't had my grandmother's house to escape to during my adolescence.

The boy I met after my parents' divorce continued to surface throughout my high school years. John had become a rather prolific drug dealer and he introduced me to my first hit of marijuana. We did pills and smoked anything that could be rolled into a Zig Zag. Drugs affected me fast and hard. I liked them because they worked immediately and were seemingly undetectable. When I drank, I wondered why it took so much more alcohol for me to get drunk than it did for my friends. They'd be passed out drunk and I would still be working at getting off. With drugs, it didn't seem to take as much to get as far.

John supplied me with drugs throughout high school. This was the 1960s when pot and love beads were the norm. I listened to the Beatles, smoked dope, drank beer and assumed everyone else was doing the same thing. Occasionally, I'd break free from John and his murky world of pipes and black lights. During these months, I'd go straight, date football players and attend parties with normal kids. It was like having a double life; one group of friends never knew the other existed.

During my junior year, my mother remarried. She was becoming desperate about our dwindling finances and the difficulties of raising three children alone. So she accepted when a cantankerous oil man from northern Montana proposed to her. On their honeymoon, they were in a snowmobile accident. She broke both of her legs; he suffered brain damage and had to have his left leg amputated at the knee.

The life-changing effect that accident had on my mother could fill a book in itself. But the result for me was easy to predict. My responsibilities doubled. I was no longer mother's best friend and partner; I was now her nurse and counselor as well. Her deranged husband resided at our house for nearly a year. He hobbled around on crutches, yelled at my brothers and barked orders at me. My mother was in leg casts up to her hips and needed constant care. A nurse's aide came in while I was at school, but at 3:30 my shift started. I learned to use coffee and cigarettes to stay awake at night and try to study.

Frequently I noticed my mother's ample supply of painkillers and sedatives. One afternoon, I took one of her blue 10 milligram Valiums. I was driving home from taking my brother somewhere when the pill hit. I had to pull off to the side of the road. My head was swimming, and my mind melted into a pool of flatness. All I wanted was sleep. I don't remember anything after that, but the euphoric recollection of that sweet oblivion never left me. I had finally discovered a drug that could stop my racing mind and silence the world around me.

After that, I dipped into her pill supply often. Eventually, she divorced my stepfather. I finally graduated from high school and went through the motions of going off to a small, religious college in Spokane, Washington. I was miserable. The loneliness was indescribable. I had gone from running a household and caring for my mother and brothers to the carefree world of living in a college dorm and listening to girls giggle about their boyfriends. Most girls would like that, but I felt totally out of place, acutely different.

A boyfriend I met the summer before college sent me frequent care packages of hashish from his army barracks in Germany. Whenever I felt especially down and sad, I would go out into the campus woods and stand in the rain to smoke the hash. By the time that slow-moving, lonely semester finally ended, I took my final exams and left Washington for good.

When I got back to Billings, I reunited with my high school friends. They were all home from the University of Montana and convinced me to go off to school with them in Missoula. Again, I went through the motions: stood in line, registered for courses, moved into a dorm, but never attended a single class. All my time was spent in John's dark Missoula apartment smoking hash, doing pills and listening to B.B. King.

The boyfriend in Germany was home on furlough and came to see me at the university. We went to the post office to pick up another care package he'd sent that I hadn't bothered to retrieve. On our way out of the post office, we were encircled by muddy Dodges and arrested by InterPol, F.B.I. and U.S. Customs agents.

The boyfriend insisted I knew nothing of the heroin in the package. And I didn't. The army colonel, former Eagle Scout and West Point cadet wound up in Leavenworth for drug smuggling. I was set free and after several sessions with a lawyer, my father arrived from Texas, and I went into a hospital to try to pull myself together. The psychiatrist at the hospital gave me a prescription for Valium and told me I needed a "series of successes." He recommended I stop associating with drug users and move to Dallas to live with my father. I did just that.

Three weeks after my arrival in Dallas, I got a wonderful job in the advertising department of Neiman-Marcus. I was never happier. Eventually I saved enough of my meager salary to rent an apartment and I rode the bus to work every day. At times I got lonely, but the apartment complex was made up of single people and we would party and drink around the pool every weekend. If pot or pills came out, I left. I had sworn off illegal drugs.

I dated frequently and enjoyed Dallas' night life. It was much more glamorous than anything I'd experienced in Montana. I noticed I could drink most of my dates under the table, and I developed the opinion that southern men just could not drink. When they tried to keep up with me, they'd wind up wrecking their cars or passed out or both. Eventually, one of them wrecked my car, too. In that accident, two passengers were seriously injured and we were taken to the Parkland Hospital emergency room. But I didn't think it was out of the ordinary to wreck a few cars and go to the hospital.

A young man named Harry came to work at Neiman's as a writer. He was funny and smart and we slowly developed a friendship. He scoffed at the idea that I was going to singles' bars with the models from work, and asked me what kind of jerks did I think I would meet in bars. It was the first time I'd ever thought about it. I quit going to the bars, but experienced terrible loneliness, alone in my one-room apartment. Suddenly, the glamorous life I thought I had became empty and monotonous. I began to have second thoughts about quitting school and trying to live the life of a twenty-five year-old when I was actually only eighteen.

Harry and I started dating. It was slow going. Unlike the other guys I had always dated, he watched his money, counted out his change and didn't drink much. I'd never dated anyone quite like him. But his wit and sensitivity, along with an incredible writing talent, kept drawing me toward him. The first ad he wrote was for heirloom china. As I sat at my desk and proofread his copy, the words pierced my heart and brought tears to my eyes.

Harry had a vulnerability about him, too, that I'd never encountered in other men. In a way, he seemed as lonely as I was, but there was something else. Little things came out—such as he hadn't been to a dentist since he was a small child. His father was well-off, but Harry didn't even have a checking account. His shoes curled up at the toes because they'd been hand-me-downs from his dad, along with his raincoat and worn—out sports jacket. On one of our early dates I gave him the first haircut he'd had in over a year. The smallest act of kindness went a long way with Harry. It was apparent to me that no one had nurtured or cared for him in a long time.

We lived together for a few months, then decided to get married. Our wedding was a hodge-podge of Neiman's co-workers and my parents who were embroiled in a vicious fight even though they were both married to other people. Harry's father was married to a young woman close to my age. She wore hot pants to the wedding and gave me a set of Tupperware bowls for a wedding present. Harry and I didn't have enough money to go on a honeymoon.

We moved into a little apartment with red carpeting and black and white rented furniture, and we were in heaven. I felt safe and sane for the first time in my life. Harry and I discovered that our childhoods were very similar. His mother had died of some mysterious illness when he was sixteen and his father was a corporate man who traveled more than he was home. Somehow, Harry managed to inject some humor into our early memories, and we agreed that we were glad we hadn't married someone from a normal family. We both had a strong sense that we finally had a home. And we were acutely aware that we had to take care of each other; no one else ever would.

I got too drunk at the office Christmas parties and once an artist from work gave me a lid of grass which Harry angrily flushed down the toilet with a stern lecture. At parties I would snort and smoke anything being passed around, and Harry often admonished me afterward. But between parties, I didn't drink, and our lives revolved around our work and each other. We were poor, but didn't know it, and we were happy.

By this time, my mother had remarried, but my second stepfather had tired of paying her hospital bills. She spent most of the last year of their brief marriage in a posh Minneapolis mental hospital. When her husband divorced her, she moved to Dallas. It was her hometown, after all. I found her a job selling dresses at Neiman's, but she rarely went to work and spent most of her time drunk at the little apartment I had located for her.

One afternoon when I went to visit her, it was obvious she'd been drinking for days and was unable to walk across the room. She begged me to go across the street and buy her a fifth of vodka at the corner liquor store. I refused and told her she'd better call AA and get sober. I don't know how I got the courage, but I told her I would never see her again if she didn't get sober. And I meant it. To my relief and astonishment, she did call AA. That summer, she got sober and has stayed sober ever since.

The following year, I started coming home from work and mixing myself some martinis before dinner. I fell in love with this potent mixture. It hit hard and fast, especially on an empty stomach. But after a few months of this, Harry once again nipped it in the bud. He told me I was starting to smell like my mother had when she drank. That did it. I quit drinking except at social occasions. He mixed my drinks from then on. They were weak Scotch and waters, and he made sure I never had more than two.

Eventually, I quit work and attended a local Jesuit university with grant money and student loans. Harry taught me how to study and I was astonished at my own capabilities. He kept reassuring me that I was smart and my grades proved him right. But my world became very small. I went to school, drove home, studied, and talked with Harry when he came home from work. I never made any friends at the university; now that I was married, college students seemed even younger and sillier than they had before. Harry was all I needed.

In 1977, my grandmother died and left us enough money to put a down payment on a house. We were thrilled. After seven years of marriage, we had longed for a house, but we could never seem to save enough for a down payment. Our new house in North Dallas was right across the street from an elementary school. We watched the children scamper on the playground and glowed with the hope of having our own soon.

On April 3, 1979, we had a healthy baby boy and named him Cameron Sage Harrison. From the start, we called him Sage and to this day, he lives up to his name. He's a wise and wonderful young man. One year after Sage's birth, I started working part-time as a writer at an advertising agency with Harry. We were making good money and when I discovered I was pregnant again, we decided to buy a bigger house in the suburbs.

On May 30th I went into labor and on June 1st, Field was born. The labor was long and difficult. An emergency cesarean section was finally ordered. They inserted an epidural into my spine but it didn't work. Next the spinal didn't work, then finally, full anesthesia was administered for the operation. Apparently, the young doctor didn't tell the nurses about the spinal and epidural; they sat me up and moved me after the operation. Later, I was plagued with blinding migraine headaches.

Worse yet, the baby almost died. He was in the ICU for several days. Finally, the neonatalogist announced that Field was well enough to take home. With the baby home, I sank into a depression that I couldn't shake. I would check and recheck the crib to make sure he was still alive. I cried uncontrollably. My OB put me on antidepressants which worked like a charm. Within three days, I was back on my feet, making cookies and as happy as Donna Reed.

The antidepressants made me drowsy during the day, so I napped every day when the babies did. This made going to sleep difficult at night, so I got some Seconal from the doctor. I tried to save those for the weekends so Harry could get up with the boys. It all seemed innocent enough.

Whenever I tried to stop the antidepressants, I felt agitated and uneasy so I started right back on them. Every so often I told myself I'd taken them long enough and tried to quit again, but I'd pick a fight with Harry or become irritable with the boys, so I put off stopping them for another few months. That cycle continued for about a year.

My headaches got progressively worse. I went to a neurologist who sympathized with my plight: two babies at home and constant pain. Over the course of several months, he gave me another prescription for antidepressants. When they failed to stop the headaches, he tried two more antidepressants on me; I didn't stop one and start another. I just took all three at once. He gave me Valium, at my request, along with Vicodan, assorted painkillers and several different sleeping pills.

Shortly after Field's birth, Harry was in a car accident and developed cluster headaches. His doctor had him come to the emergency room for a shot of Demerol. I watched Harry's body relax and his pain disappear. Seeing the effect the narcotic had on him was like watching an old lover walk into the room. I longed for that sweet oblivion.

When the pills failed to help my daily headaches, I too went to the emergency rooms at local hospitals for shots of Demerol. After two years of this, my worst fear came true: the Demerol stopped working. One afternoon I got a shot and nothing happened. The ER doctors gave me another one and sent me home. I felt slightly sleepy. This infuriated me. Nothing worked anymore. I was taking pills all the time. First thing in the morning and last thing at night. I never went anywhere without Valium and Vicodan in my purse and in my pockets. But it didn't seem that I could feel the effects of them anymore.

I took three kinds of antidepressants and was depressed all the time. I gulped several sleeping pills at night along with constant doses of 10 milligram Valium and couldn't sleep. Sometimes I was afraid if I did go to sleep I would stop breathing from all the sedatives. So I paced around the house and called all-night pharmacies to find out if there was an antidote for sedative overdose. The nightmare had begun.

For three years this went on. I kept my house clean, my children were fed and bathed. I did any necessary driving in the mornings while I was still semi-alert. And I didn't tell a soul how many pills I was taking. Not even Harry. Not even myself. I was active in the church women's organization and when someone would call me about an upcoming meeting or something that had to be done, I would take notes during the conversation; otherwise I forgot every word.

Dates got mixed up, appointments missed, but I tried as hard as I could to keep up. I was terrified to load the boys up in their car seats and take them anywhere. I knew I'd either get lost or have an accident. So I drove dangerously slow, bouncing off curbs and taking side streets whenever possible. Expressways terrified me. Toward the end I never went anywhere.

Into the fourth year, I was taking more and more pills. I'd forget if I'd taken a pill, so I'd take another. The doctor kept prescribing more and more since nothing seemed to be working. Finally, I went into the hospital for a headache that would not relent. They were very sparing with Demerol, which enraged me. The pills stopped coming. On the tenth day, I was hallucinating from drug withdrawal.

The doctors were scratching their heads trying to figure out what was wrong with me. Psychologists paraded into my room with their inkblot tests and MMPI's. My liver was failing, and I kept hallucinating. By that time, my mother had been in recovery for several years. She'd seen just about everything and she'd kept quiet long enough. She suggested to the doctors that if they gave me some Valium, I'd stop hallucinating. It worked. They sent me home with a schedule of decreasing doses to wean myself off Valium. They had no idea that was only the tip of the iceberg.

I went home from the hospital, but had to go back that same afternoon. Convulsions were wracking my body and I was urinating blood. I knew I was dying. Harry stood by my hospital bed that entire night and held my hand. I thought if he let go of my hand for a split second, my soul would leave. I was dying and I knew it.

They gave me shots and pills and sent me home. They probably thought I was a nut case.

After a few days at home, the withdrawals started again. My mother finally convinced Harry that I was indeed coming off drugs and needed to go to a drug treatment center. That afternoon was hell. I fought off any suggestion of a treatment center. I could do it myself. Because I was too weak to lift a fork, Harry spoonfed me. The psychosis brought on by the drug withdrawal was becoming acute. Fortunately, my mother came over and took care of my boys who, by then, had found the magic markers and covered our beige velvet couch in black ink.

My mother told Harry and me, in no uncertain terms, that I would die of convulsions in front of my children if I didn't get into a treatment center immediately. Earlier in the year, Harry filmed a commercial for a new treatment center nearby, so I shakily gathered up some clean underwear and left for the treatment center that night. I was wearing black pedal pushers and a pajama top and figured I'd be back home in a day or two.

As usual, I filled my pockets and purse with pills when we left the house. And I took a Halcion for good measure as we walked out the door. I was shaking and twitching and rocking back and forth in the front seat of our car. When we finally arrived at the drug treatment facility out in the country, I shuffled like an old woman through the foggy parking lot, leaning heavily on Harry's arm.

Once inside, we were quick to point out to the admitting nurse that I was indeed having some problems, which was obvious, but I was very reluctant to adopt or accept the label of "drug addict." Drug addicts were not young mothers who lived in the suburbs, were they? The male nurse shook his head agreeably. Then, that saint of a man gave me three Valium tablets. I greedily swallowed them and thought maybe this wouldn't be so bad after all.

About twenty minutes later, we finished the paperwork. My uncontrollable rocking and shaking had stopped. I was calm and quite rational. The fact that I was more lucid on drugs than off got Harry's attention. It felt as if he and the nurse were sharing some inside joke about me. I didn't understand it; all I knew was that I felt immeasurably better. I was willing to spend one night in this place as long as they kept dosing me with Valium. Then I'd go back home.

For twenty-eight days, I stayed at that treatment center. They stopped the Valium and gave me four phenobarb tablets every day to prevent convulsions. In the meantime, Harry cleaned out the house and found eighty working prescriptions of pills hidden in cabinets and drawers. He brought them to the treatment center in a shopping bag, where they were promptly tossed in the trash. I couldn't conceive of throwing pills away. I was furious at him for doing this. I thought I'd just have to spend all that time and money again to get the prescriptions refilled.

Harry attended every meeting and class they told him to and when he found out I had taken some sleeping pills smuggled in to me at the treatment center by a patient, he hit the roof. Harry was no longer in denial. He was convinced I was a drug addict. I felt totally alone and betrayed by my best friend. Harry had always stood by me and now he was against me. He and the boys drove out to the treatment center every Sunday after church. They ate lunch with me in the center's cafeteria; then Sage and Field romped around the grounds while Harry and I talked. These visits were painful because I missed the boys terribly, but the idea of going home and taking care of them terrified me. The treatment center never let me go home on a weekend pass. They said I would find a way to use drugs if I went home.

When I was finally able to make it through a twenty-four hour period without the phenobarb, I called my mother to come and get me out of treatment. I hated it in that place. They kept telling me I was a drug addict and that I would be dead within a year. Harry was the good guy and I was the bad one. He was soaking up the information, they said, like a sponge, and I was defiant and angry. I would never make it, they claimed. Spotting my obvious dependence on Harry, one counselor even suggested that I would have to get a divorce in order to break my addiction to Harry as well as drugs. They recommended I go to a halfway house back east somewhere for several more months. If I went home, my prognosis was not good.

When my mother arrived for me, I dragged my belongings out to the parking lot in a plastic trash bag and tossed them into the backseat of her car. She took me straight to a Twelve Step recovery meeting near my house. I was expecting people from under the bridge, but I saw women who looked like they'd just left a PTA meeting. They were nicely dressed and pretty. Afterward, these same ladies took me to lunch and one of them told me to come back to hear a speaker that night. She looked straight into my eyes and said, "Listen for the similarities, not the differences. Then you'll get better."

The doctor who ran the treatment center had said something similar to me that same morning. He told me that if I ever let myself feel, I might recover. Two important truths had been given to me by these individuals, both of whom were recovering addicts themselves, and because I trusted their experience, I was willing to take their suggestions. Harry wouldn't protect me anymore. I didn't have my pills. This had to work. I had run out of ideas, and I was powerless. My life had truly become unmanageable.

My marriage was turned upside down by the realization that I was a drug addict. Harry had always been my champion, my warrior. Whenever I had a problem, I knew he could solve it for me. He was loyal to a fault and up to this point in our relationship, he trusted me implicitly. But the fabric of our marriage was torn apart now. My loyal guardian had betrayed me by ignoring my pleas that I was not a drug addict. He had agreed with the people who ran the treatment center that I was undoubtedly a drug addict and had handed over a shopping bag full of pills to confirm it. Then, during family week, he had listed several instances where my addiction had interfered with our family life. Telling these things aloud in front of my mother, other patients and staff members of the center broke the primary code of our addicted marriage: always keep the secrets.

Harry was not going to fix me anymore, and it infuriated me. When I had a problem, and sometimes just making cereal was a major problem, he would either ignore me or tell me to go to a meeting. Likewise, if something broke around the house or one of the children had a crisis, he stepped back and made me handle it on my own. Whenever I tried to pick a fight with him, he put on his jogging shoes and trotted out the front door. At night when I paced and smoked until dawn, he didn't console and comfort me; he went to bed and slept! Instead of being grateful to him for allowing me to break my dependency on him and cultivate my own coping skills, I hated him. He was abandoning me in my time of greatest need. Harry comprehended long before I did that no human power could relieve my drug addiction. He could not repair my damaged system. That job was now between me and my God.

STEP TWO. Came to believe that a Power greater than ourselves could restore us to sanity.

*W*hen I was twelve years old, my father decided he wanted to leave Montana and move to a small east Texas town about thirty miles from Dallas. He planned to take over a sizable cotton farm which had been in my mother's family for generations. This undertaking turned into a disaster and my parents separated shortly thereafter; but the one interesting feature of that little town was the state mental hospital which sprawled behind a high fence a few miles from our home.

Visitors were allowed on weekends and occasionally, at my urging, we drove through the grounds, more out of curiosity than anything else. I stared up at the patients who stood in the open windows. Their fingers were entwined around the wire screens and they stared blankly down at the carloads of arriving families. On the hottest days, the "nuts" would stand in front of the windows nude. It was the only breeze they got in the unairconditioned wards.

Those haunting images of that state hospital lingered with me forever. A fear that stalked my mind was that I would end up locked in a back ward of a mental hospital someday. I always suspected that my thinking was different from other people's. If I ever dared to say what I was thinking, people sometimes would stare at me a little too long. So I usually kept my thoughts to myself. I was terrified someone would eventually discover this terrible secret in me and lock me away. For good.

Today that fear hasn't disappeared, but it has taken its proper place in my consciousness. I know that the locked back ward is my future if I return to drugs and I'm not lucky enough to die. My mind will disintegrate. I know this because I came perilously close to it when I tried to stop taking drugs on my own. I'll never forget the feeling of losing my mind, of seeing things that weren't there, of hearing voices of people who didn't exist. Some people say when you're crazy you don't know it, but I knew it.

The first few months after treatment, I believed I had been a better person on drugs. I was certainly a lot calmer while on drugs. With the tranquilizers and sedatives gone, it felt like my brain overfired at every impulse. Messages didn't have to fight their way through the muck of sedation anymore. I frequently felt like an over-stimulated infant: quick to cry, nervous, exhausted and irritable.

It didn't help that I could only sleep a few hours at night. Whatever sleep rhythms I had before taking drugs were long gone from the overuse of sleeping pills. I lay awake at night, wandered around the house, smoked cigarettes and wondered if things would ever get any better. I felt as though my transmission was in park, but someone was constantly pushing down on the accelerator. I was revved up but paralyzed by fears.

In the midst of this turmoil, I continued to go to recovery meetings every day. The expression, "Suit up and show up," had new meaning for me, along with, "Bring the body and the mind will follow." All my hopes hung on the Second Step; I felt insane and was desperate to change. Everyone at the recovery meetings appeared calm and comfortable with their lives. In contrast, my foot tapped incessantly on the chair in front of me, I was racing internally, my mind flitted from one thing to the next, and I became incensed at the slightest provocation. Driving to and from the meetings, I clutched my steering wheel and cried to God to please restore me to sanity. I couldn't stand this anymore!

Because I was insane, my marriage was crazy too. I would go in and out of rage, shift from anger to infantile weeping within the same second. I wanted Harry to spend every waking minute with me; then when he tried, I accused him of being too intrusive and critical. I wanted to be home, but when I was home, I wanted to leave. I was like a person with an injury who can't find a comfortable position.

The way I worked Step Two helped me tremendously. My sponsor had me list all the ways that I felt insane. That was easy. Normal people didn't have panic attacks and make suicide plans at the thought of going to their sons' swim meet. I discovered I was afraid of just about everything, especially people. But the healing came in the second part of Step Two. I was told to write down my ideal for myself, what kind of woman I would like to be when I was restored to sanity.

I painstakingly described what I wanted to be like, what my picture of myself would be as a sane wife and mother. There would be no rage and no fear. I would have order, both externally and internally. Serenity would be the norm rather than the exception, and I would behave rationally, no matter what the circumstances. My sponsor assured me I would be restored to my ideal of sanity and would have these things, but first I had to work all the steps and try to act sane even when I didn't feel like it. In other words, I had to act my way into right thinking; addicts simply cannot do it the other way around.

Prior to being introduced to the Twelve Steps, I thought that if I could arrange my surroundings and the people in it to be the way I wanted them to be, then I would feel peace of mind. Serenity and calm would come if we had more money. Fears would vanish if Harry didn't push me to do so much. My stress was a by-product of the fighting between my two sons. If they would stop, I could feel better. These were old ideas; the results, as they say, were nil. It wasn't the world's job to adapt to me; it became my task to learn to adapt to the world, stressful as it was. Sanity would have to be sought in an environment where money was short, and kids fought.

There were two prongs to my insanity which had to be dealt with immediately. The first was my belief that I was a better person on drugs. That was a lie my addicted mind told me and the only way to dispel it was to begin to take note and appreciate the benefits, both large and small, of being clean and sober.

My son, Sage, was in first grade during this time in my recovery. His class had finished studying the family unit and he brought home a portrait he had shown the class of his family. The crayon drawing outlined his dad, little brother and himself swimming in a pool. I was not in the picture. Admittedly, I had been away almost two months in the hospital and the treatment center. Before that, I spent as much of my day as possible in bed. Toward the end of my addiction, I had retreated so far into myself that I had practically disappeared. His family drawing was painfully accurate.

When I saw that drawing, one part of me said, what's the use? Why am I trying to stay sober and be a mother? But fortunately, the part that was striving for sanity won out. I began participating more in family activities. When Harry and the boys loaded up to go somewhere, I pushed aside my fears and forced myself to go along. Once a week, I took hamburgers up to their elementary school and joined them for lunch in the school cafeteria. I participated in dinner conversations, made meals and tried my level best to be a part of their lives.

Soon, the little moments with them made me grateful to be sober. I could remember conversations from the day before. They got to their soccer practices and school events on the right day and at the right time. I learned what their favorite foods were and things they liked to do. If I knew all that before treatment, I had forgotten it by the time I got home.

Toward the end of the school year, Sage brought home another picture of his family. I braced myself against the kitchen counter as I unfolded the stiff construction paper, assuring myself it was okay if I wasn't in the picture. But I was there in bright yellow crayon with a big smile on my face. There was a mother in his family, and it was me!

Most of the things that happened the last two years before sobriety were lost to me. During my first year in recovery, movies came on TV that I'd seen a year or two earlier at the theater, but forgotten. People would stop me in a mall or outside church and talk to me like I was their best friend, but I had no idea who they were. It was embarrassing, but I learned to fake recognition and accepted these memory lapses. Eventually, it became amusing.

Aside from my children, I discovered little things in myself that I could be grateful for. The withdrawal symptoms were unwanted guests throughout the first year, but gradually they lessened and diminished. I didn't continually tap my foot anymore. I had developed an involuntary hand-wringing habit that came when I stopped drugs. One day I looked down at my hands and they were still. Each little improvement gave me renewed hope.

After nine months of insomnia, I finally slept for a full seven hours. That was a Godsend and the real beginning of sanity. I gradually settled into a daily routine of eating meals at mealtime, whether I was hungry or not, and I usually wasn't. Every morning, I'd greet the neighbors as they got their morning papers while I walked for thirty minutes trying to sweat out more of the drug residue. This daily structure helped restore my sleep patterns, and it is a routine which I still follow today.

The second deadly prong of my insanity was a yearning to kill myself. This thought would creep into my mind and I could not dismiss it. My mind wanted me dead. Finally I learned what to do when this obsession came. I would pray for all the angels, all the power in the universe, to come to my aid and keep me from killing myself.

I forced myself to call my sponsor when I started feeling the need to die. By the time I called her, I usually had the kids at the babysitter's and was ready to carry out the deed. But she always talked me down and we prayed for the angels to intervene. After five years of struggling with this compulsion, I think it has finally left me.

My husband and my sponsor both convinced me that there are times when I cannot believe anything my mind is telling me. Being alone with my mind is like going behind enemy lines. I could get killed.

My first experience with sanity was after eighteen months of sobriety. I was in a Twelve Step meeting, not the one I usually attended. They had several phrases framed on the wall. One stated in bold black letters, "We will know peace of mind." I thought for a minute. My mind was at peace. It wasn't racing. It wasn't torturing me with death calls. The promises of sobriety were coming true; maybe there was hope. Peace of mind was what I wanted from pills and painkillers. I savored the last moment on Demerol right before passing out. That was the closest I ever came to having peace of mind prior to sobriety.

Being restored to sanity was my goal for the first few years of sobriety. I stopped calling myself crazy. I didn't let my husband call me crazy or nuts, even as a joke. Those words were banned from our household. I was working hard to be sane; it wasn't something I took for granted. I did everything I could do to maintain level thinking and sanity. A combination of daily recovery meetings, walking, eating, and sleeping resulted in a slow but steady increase in serenity and sanity.

One day I called my sponsor and hurriedly told her I felt crazy. She interrupted my diatribe and said firmly, "You are not crazy. You have been restored to sanity." To this day, no one has ever paid me a higher compliment.

Beautiful, screwed up women are a dime a dozen. If they're flamboyant, loud or have to be the center of attention, I silently bless them, but I avoid them. To be a safe, sane woman was, and still is, my ideal. I avoid angry people; women who claim to be victims of one system or another. I don't read books or see movies about neurotic women. I've been there, done that; it's a rough road. And, crazy attracts crazy.

Today, I seek out men and women who have a drug-free spiritual life, help others and function in a sane manner. I try to emulate them. I ask them how they pray, what they read, where their paths to serenity lie. And I follow them. These people don't come along often. Sometimes their paths don't suit me. But the few people who have been spiritual guides for me have given me untold gifts which help keep me sane.

I learned that there is a power greater than myself whom I choose to call God. He puts people in my path to guide me through life, not to avoid pitfalls, but to handle them without having to use drugs or kill myself. I may not do it gracefully and I certainly do not suffer in silence, but with the help of God and my friends, I've learned I can live life on life's terms. And I think that's what sanity is about.

STEP THREE. Made a decision to turn our will and our lives over to the care of God *as we understood Him.*

I was raised in the Episcopal Church and I always believed in God. My image of him was of a peaceful man who stood in a lily field and blessed people who behaved themselves. He wasn't mean or condemning; he loved people, good people, but he wasn't powerful either. And when the going got tough, he got going. He was a nice guy but rarely there when I needed him. When I wrote out that concept of God and showed it to my sponsor, she said it was no wonder I was reluctant to turn my life and my will over to his care. This guy might lose it!

I needed another God. The crux of Step Three is that we turn our lives and our will over to the care of God as we understand him. First of all, I needed the right understanding of God. That can come from a church or a spiritual leader. In my case, it came from my sponsor and two years of voracious reading on the subject. Previously, I had turned my life and will over to the care of drugs. Now I had to find a God that would stick with me, one that I could trust and who was all powerful. I had to let go of relying on my own power. It had taken me down too far.

Initially, I changed my image of God. He got older, wiser, more worldly. In my imagination, he smoked a cigar and listened patiently to me as we sat on a park bench together. I would close my eyes and see myself sitting with this new God, telling him all my troubles and asking him for help. I finally got close enough to see who he really was: George Burns! Admittedly that was unusual, but this was my first attempt at having a personal relationship with God, and George Burns was the best I could do.

I had this "George Burns God" for at least a year. Maybe longer. Sometimes I wrote out my problems on a piece of paper and put them in a glass case I called my God Box. I imagined George Burns reading the piece of paper and, believe it or not, that gave me peace. I hoped this new God would do something about the problems I inserted into the God Box. And sure enough he did. Things started to improve.

Slowly I developed a trust in God, a God who wasn't going to leave me when the going got tough. Similarly, I began trusting people too. I think as my trust in people increased, so did my trust in God. I started to really believe that people cared about me, that I mattered in their lives. For fifteen years I was sure that Harry would leave me any day. Now I actually believed he would stay.

I cannot develop a spiritual faith by sitting at home reading recovery books. I have to be around people who sincerely care about me; who know me thoroughly—and who, even after they know me, still love me. That's where I often feel God's love—through people.

Another avenue I traveled that helped me to understand God's love was through my love for my children. When they made mistakes, I didn't call them stupid and tell them they would be better off dead. That's what my mind had told *me* when *I* fouled up. I reassured my children that it was human to make a mistake; I didn't love them any less. They could learn from it and go on. I tried to start treating myself with the same compassion that I did my sons. Instead of chastising myself, I would say out loud, "You just messed up. Now you know not to do it that way again." And I understood that God's love for me was even more profound and forgiving than any human love I could experience.

I started to feel overwhelmed with gratitude for the smallest things in my life. Friends were in my life—not dozens, but a few dear men and women who sincerely loved me, even on my bad days. My children were blossoming and healthy. Sunlight no longer caused me to wince; it lit up my home. I was no longer afraid to answer the telephone or go to the mailbox. I didn't avoid people. Financial problems came, but they somehow always managed to work themselves out. God's power was apparent to me in the simplest, most exquisite ways.

I don't know when, but eventually George Burns receded, and I simply felt the most amazing love and peace when I closed my eyes every morning and tried to make a conscious contact with God. He wasn't on a park bench anymore. He was in my heart. He was in the voices of my friends and the sweet hugs from my children. He was, in fact, everywhere.

God was in my marriage as well. Instead of seeing the flaws in Harry, I began to see the many ways he blessed my life. I no longer resented him when he asked me to do something for or with him. Instead, I appreciated his high energy level and his willingness to include me in his many endeavors. My critical nature had prevented me from seeing the great effort Harry was putting into his own recovery; how he was working the steps and trying as hard as I was to change destructive behaviors. I had been so consumed by my own private pain, that I had not seen the anguish he must have suffered in letting go of me and turning me over to strangers to bring me back from the jaws of addiction. It took great courage and trust in God for him to do that.

Just as I had turned my life and my will over to the care of God as I understood him, I did the same with my marriage. Wiser people than I had advised me not to "work" on my marriage; God would do that. It was just my job, they told me, to stay sober and act decently. Something as simple as using good manners in a marriage makes a big difference: politely answering a question when asked; saying please and thank you like you would with any friend; eliminating all sarcasm from my conversations with Harry. These small things went a long, long way in making major repairs in our relationship.

There is a park across the street from my house and every morning I walk its two-mile perimeter. A creek winds through the center of the park, and at one spot near its banks, two mature oak trees grow about forty feet apart. Unlike the surrounding oaks, these two trees bend toward each other forming the most extraordinary arch. It's almost human the way their branches reach toward one another, straining for contact. If I were to give my relationship with God a visual symbol it would be those two trees. At all times, even in storms and high winds, God is leaning toward me. If I remember to reach toward him, all is well.

STEP FOUR. Made a searching and fearless moral inventory of ourselves.

*W*e're only as sick as our secrets, and drug addicts have plenty of secrets. I had so many secrets, in fact, that I even kept some of them from myself. Making the moral inventory described in Step Four doesn't consist of sitting down and thinking about what my moral victories and defeats are. As part of my first Fourth Step, I had to write out every resentment I could recall, every fear I harbored, and explore how I really felt about sex. I discovered that a great deal of power and insight comes from putting a pen to paper.

My resentments went as far back as my first grade teacher. I wrote out why I resented some people, and what my part was in the problem. The resentments usually had to do with my security (money) or my self-esteem and/or ego. When I looked up the word resentment, I discovered that it meant to re-feel something with displeasure—year after year. As I listed my resentments, I realized I was re-feeling anger at dozens of people; these were resentments I had harbored for decades.

I had to be fearless and thorough. I couldn't leave one resentment off that list. If I could remember it, could re-feel it, chances were I had not forgiven that person or myself for the original incident. Bottled up anger and hatred saps the spirit and can be deadly for a drug addict or alcoholic. There were people I felt I shouldn't be angry with, even though I was—my parents, my husband, even my children. But this list wasn't for publication; it was for my recovery. I had to be honest and write out the people I felt resentment toward, and disregard whether I should or shouldn't feel the way I did. When I completed my list of resentments, it was striking how much anger I had been carrying around with me over the years. No wonder I needed painkillers!

After completion of my resentments a pattern had emerged, and it became obvious to me that I had let one element poison every relationship I ever had. That element was fear. I was too afraid to say how I was feeling or to ask for what I wanted. People were supposed to be able to read my mind. I could not be honest. If they were doing something that hurt my feelings—like making fun of me, or lying to me—instead of asking them to stop, I simply abandoned the relationship. I left several confused friends and family members wondering why I disappeared out of their lives.

Fear merits its own section in the Fourth Step. I listed all my fears, and there were many. I had constant fear of my children or myself getting some terrible illness; I was afraid Harry would leave me; I was afraid we'd go broke and lose everything; I was afraid to drive on expressways. Cats frightened me. The list goes on and on. Those fears had taken on a life of their own and robbed me from enjoying the present moment. I was constantly anticipating some disaster, whether real or imagined. And since disasters always loomed in the future, that's where I lived. Never in the present moment.

I learned that the best way to neutralize fear is to talk about it with someone. This takes the power out of the fear. I have to muster all my mental discipline in order to stay in the present moment. I know that if my mind creeps ahead into future territory, I'll meet up with the monsters of fear again, and miss out on any gifts that may come my way today.

Prior to recovery, I lost years out of my life to fear and the habit of living in the future. When my children were babies I constantly anticipated their next meal, their next nap. I would have their lunch made before they were even hungry and I'd have them down for a nap before they yawned. If they cried, I was sure they were sick. While they were still infants, I worried that they wouldn't be smart enough to pass the SAT's. I rarely sat back and enjoyed the moment with my children. When they crawled, I wanted them to walk. When they walked, I wanted them to go to school. I was always scurrying and scampering, trying to stay one step ahead of some unforeseen crisis. This constant flirtation with the future is a surefire way to stay on edge and afraid.

I did the same thing with my marriage. The minute something good came our way, I'd start worrying about what we'd do if and when we lost it. For example, when we moved into our new house, I didn't let myself become too attached to it; after all, Harry might lose his job and we'd have to move into an apartment somewhere. When we went on vacation, I'd start talking about what we should do on our next vacation. If Harry got a promotion, I'd find some article in the paper about an advertising company that went bankrupt and I'd imagine the same thing happening to Harry's company. I simply couldn't stay out of the future. This awareness came to me when I worked the Fourth Step.

Once resentments and fears are covered, the Fourth Step requires a sexual inventory. I listed the men with whom I'd had sexual relations, both real and imagined. I had to examine where I'd been selfish, dishonest or inconsiderate. Sometimes I caused jealousy and hurt feelings, mostly stemming from the inability, on my part, to be honest in the relationship. Again, I almost never verbalized my feelings. If things got uncomfortable, I simply abandoned the relationship with little or no explanation.

The second facet of this sexual inventory was redemptive. It involved writing out what my ideal scenario was: how I would like to behave and participate in a healthy sexual relationship. I wanted to be trusting, uninhibited, and receptive. At the same time, I wanted to be a safe and an understanding wife—not demanding. I wanted to be trustworthy and loyal. This meant that I would not flirt with other men; I would not stir up jealousy within my marriage. Flirtations, no matter how harmless, can often cause hurt feelings.

When I saw this ideal on paper, I realized it was not an impossible task at all. I had it within me to be all these things. But I had to start by being honest with my husband, tell him if I was upset by something he said or did. I had to say no when I felt no, and try to set fear outside our relationship, or it would corrode our marriage thoroughly. I tried with every ounce of mental discipline I could draw upon to stay in the present moment, and not to let my mind and my imagination wander into dark caverns of the past or the future where I didn't belong. My reality was good, and I had to practice staying in it.

My basic fear was, as I said before, that Harry would wake up one day and leave me. I couldn't eliminate that thought, but I was able to put it outside the relationship and when it tried to intrude, I would tell myself that I'd think about it later. So I wasn't killing off the thought, just postponing it. But inevitably I'd notice how Harry had done something loving, and I'd realize he had no intention of leaving me. As more and more of these affirmations accumulated, my fear become less persistent.

By keeping fears at bay and being truthful with myself and others, my ideal has come true for me. I am a trustworthy wife. I don't lie about where I'm going, what I'm spending or what I need. I sometimes have to muster every ounce of courage to do these things, but the old ways are fading. And by looking toward my ideal, I know what I want to be and I try, to the best of my ability, to embody the attributes of my own ideals. Most days, I'm sure I have become the kind of woman God intended me to be.

At first, the Fourth Step sounded like an overwhelming task, but I knew I had to be willing to go to any lengths to stay sober. The Fourth Step had to be done if I was to stay off drugs. Writing out all these things was a humbling experience, but it cast a healing light on the dark secrets I'd harbored in my mind that caused innumerable problems and contortions of my soul.

STEP FIVE. Admitted to God, to ourselves and to another human being the exact nature of our wrongs.

*M*any religions call for a confession to cleanse the soul. That is what Step Five is about. After writing out Step Four, I sat down with another woman who was in recovery and, item by item, read her everything I had written. As I shared, she shared. Many of my actions which I thought were most humiliating and embarrassing, she had experienced as well. The mutuality of our shared experiences and feelings was like balm to a wound.

The most amazing part of doing Step Five was that I felt no judgment, no condemnation on the listener's part. I didn't need that; I had already condemned myself many times over. Instead, by airing these deep dark secrets, I had made room in my soul for God to come in and begin his healing. The healing started when this woman sitting across from me would nod in complete understanding as I was revealing myself to her.

Possibly the reason this had such a profound effect was that this was the first time I had ever let another human being see and know all of me. I had always been the type of person who could sit and listen to someone else's problems by the hour, but I was careful to never let them know too much about me. This time I couldn't afford any reservations. I couldn't hide anything or leave out some shameful item. All was revealed, and my friend just smiled and nodded and accepted me, flaws and all.

I was free. For once, I felt like a member of the human race. I could look anyone in the eye and not be ashamed. My deeds were not extraordinarily bad or good. I was just a human being, like other people. That was an enormous relief for me. I'd felt different all my life. I was either better or worse, and always separate from others. My guilt and shame had separated me from everyone I knew. And now, by spending a few hours revealing myself, good and bad, the guilt and shame were gone. I no longer had to compare myself to others.

Another benefit of completing my Fifth Step was that patterns in my behavior seemed to stand out on the paper like a design in bas-relief. My inability to be honest was something I never saw before taking the Fifth Step. It was quickly apparent that I repeated behaviors throughout my life which always led to the same consequences. By seeing that, I was relieved of ever having to do them again. I didn't have to keep making those same mistakes over and over again.

Because that woman, and several since then, accepted me thoroughly, just as I was, I began to believe that others could accept me as well. I started to see that I wasn't the only one in the universe who had messed up on frequent occasions. To be accepted by even just one person who knew me so thoroughly freed me tremendously.

I mistakenly held the belief most of my life that people would only love me if I was good. I tried hard to be perfect, but always fell short of the mark. I was convinced everyone saw me as a failure. Experiencing the Fifth Step made me realize that I don't love people more because of their marvelous accomplishments. My soul stirs inside me when people tell me about their struggles, and admit their true feelings. If they honestly reveal their defeats and express their fears, I instinctively respond to them and will do anything within my power to support them. It is by helping others, responding to their needs, that I get better.

This new awareness—that I was acceptable, even though I wasn't perfect—helped my marriage as well. I thought Harry was holding me up to some unattainable standard of wifedom. I had to score a hundred on the wife test, or he'd leave me. I didn't know I could be inept or admit my fears and still be accepted. Being straightforward with one person gave me the courage to be truthful about my inner concerns with Harry.

If I didn't want to go to a client party, I told Harry how it terrified me. Before working the Fifth Step, I would have gone to the party and then have become enraged over some unrelated incident, or pretended to be fine when I was far from it. Usually, by talking about them, the fears subsided. Through these discussions with Harry, I discovered he wasn't holding me up to any standard; I was the one who demanded perfection from myself! When I began to get honest with Harry, I saw that he too struggled, and that we both needed to listen and support each other on our journeys. Many of the things that I was afraid of frightened him as well. The things I hated doing, he didn't really enjoy either. Listening with an open mind, free from judgment or criticism, is the kindest gift anyone can give to another.

When I'm talking to God, I feel that he is giving me his full attention. This can be true in all loving relationships, whether it's with a best friend or a husband, when we give our undivided attention and listen with our whole heart, just as God does. Whenever I talk to my sponsor, I know she is giving me her complete attention. The day I did my Fifth Step with her, she listened intently, with absolutely no judgmentalism. I felt her love and acceptance for me melt away the walls I had built between myself and the rest of humanity. That same unconditional love and sense of utter safety is what I now try to bring to my marriage.

Every year since 1985, I've worked the steps. The Fourth and Fifth Steps are much shorter for me now, so they're easier to write. I do this because it keeps me current. I no longer walk around harboring resentments for years on end. Fears don't fester and grow. This cleansing process is not something I look forward to, and it's never easy, but the results are always worth the effort. I never again want to feel isolated and different from others. I like holding my head up and being a contributing member of my community. Likewise, I don't want last year's insult or injured feelings to color this year's affections toward Harry or anyone else. If I'm carrying a resentment or jealousy, it needs to be written down, discussed and given over to God. Sometimes sharing it with a third party is enough to take the power out of it; other times, I need to make amends or talk it over with Harry. Either way, I want to keep our relationship as free from resentment and dishonesty as possible.

STEP SIX. Were entirely ready to have God remove all these defects of character.

*A*fter sharing my Fourth and Fifth Steps, my character defects were easy to recognize. My fear of being honest with people became obvious. I had misconceptions about how people judged me. I was plagued with fear, jealousy, loneliness and a wide array of insecurities. The list seemed to go on and on. I thought the whole situation might be hopeless. The character defect which was most apparent throughout the reading of my Fifth Step was self-hate. My feelings were never as important as other people's. My wants were not as valid. Deep inside, I honestly doubted if I deserved to breathe the same air as others.

Early in my recovery, I went to church with my young family and looked around at the other women sitting calmly in the pews. Their minds seemed to be at peace. They weren't tapping their foot or glancing around the room like a caged animal, the way I was. My mind told me that any one of these women could make a better wife and mother for my family than I could. The self-hate consumed me. I felt like I was contaminating the church.

Step Six seemed like the perfect stopping point for people like me, who liked to contemplate their flaws. For too many months I had steeped myself in this self-deprecation. Every mistake I made, I magnified in my mind to reinforce my dreadful self-concept. I was quick to add new ones to my list of defects, thcn shake my head, knowing God could never remove these flaws in my character. Depression, thoughts of suicide, utter despair followed as I catalogued my faults and wallowed in Step Six. My tendency toward self-destruction was running at full tilt. Without hope, depression is inevitable.

Finally, someone pointed out to me that I made this step entirely too complicated. It wasn't supposed to be a stopping-off point where I punished myself indefinitely until one day God would magically transform me into a perfect person. All the step says is that we are ready to have God remove our defects. No more, no less.

Was I ready to have the defects removed? Yes.

I had to move on to the next steps that day.

Today when I work this step, I don't linger long. But I use it for what it is: a step which demands humility and self-honesty. It's a mirror, not a magnifying glass, of who I really am, good and bad. I've always been quick to accept the bad in me, but now I try to accept the good qualities I possess as well.

Ironically, what I consider my worst defect is often an asset as well. For example, I may have trouble being honest with someone, but I'm also gentle with people and rarely hurt their feelings. My perfectionism can cause me untold distress, but I can be depended on to get a job done. I've discovered the same is true for others. I have one son who is constantly disorganized, but his worry-free spirit enables him to have a kind heart and sunny disposition. My husband loses things constantly and is totally absent-minded, but his creative genius has financially supported us for over twenty years and his enthusiasm for life is limitless. Therefore, if I'm focusing on someone's character defect, I try to remember to turn the coin over and see the other side, which is usually a God-given gift in their personality which sets them apart from all others.

I am quick to get beyond Step Six. I finish my Fifth Step, jot down the character defects which led me to hurt myself or others, then move immediately to the Seventh Step. Never again do I want to experience the level of depression and self-absorption that I inflicted upon myself in the past by incorrectly working this step.

STEP SEVEN. Humbly asked Him to remove our shortcomings.

*T*hat was easy. I got down on my knees and asked God to remove the character defects which had demanded so much of my attention over several weeks. Then it occurred to me that he didn't need my precious list. God was all too aware of my failings. It wasn't necessary for me to recite them.

I no sooner asked God to remove these defects than I was hit in the face by one of my major defects: jealousy. I had felt a sudden surge of envy when a close friend told me that her parents were giving her son new clothes for school.

My two boys were starting school and we barely had enough money to buy them new shoes. My hospital expenses were insurmountable. In addition, I had written several hot checks before treatment, which the bank covered, but we had to repay. Life was not treating me fairly! Why didn't I have parents who would help me out?

So there I was, full of jealousy and self-pity. What should I do about these defects?

First, I asked God to remove them.

Second, I acted as if he had.

Instead of contemplating life's woes, I got busy helping someone else. A young mother who lived in our community asked my help in getting her off speed and cocaine. As I spent long hours and several evenings talking with her, the problem of the school clothes seemed to shrink in size. By the time I convinced my friend she needed to be hospital-ized, school started. Being a typical August in Texas, it was a hundred degrees in the shade. My sons would have refused to wear a stiff new pair of jeans anyway. They were happy to bound out of the house in new sneakers and their baggy summer shorts. By October, when it got cool and they needed them, we could afford new clothes.

My shortcomings, no matter what they are, will invari-ably interfere with my helping others. They always rise to the fore whenever I'm hurried, hassled and overly involved with my own little world. At those times, I get angry if my children ask me to do one more thing; I'm abrupt with a sales clerk if he's moving too slowly. Waiting has never been easy for me. When I'm stressed, impatience rears its ugly head, and I can't even take the time to fill my car with gas. I fuss and fume like I'm the CEO of some major cor-poration, when all I really have to do is get groceries for dinner.

Character defects always stem from self-pity and a defeating sense of hopelessness. They will come up until the day I die, but now when I recognize my faults, I don't dwell on them. I simply slow down and ask God to remove them, act as if he has, then turn my attention to doing something for someone else. This could be something as simple as making tunafish sandwiches for the new family moving in across the street. Or it could be as complicated as following a map to drive to an unsafe part of town to sit with an indigent woman in a charity detox center. I've done both; the results were equally gratifying.

The simple message about Step Seven is that we *all* have character defects. I have to become willing to let God remove mine. He is all powerful and he will remove them when he thinks I am capable of handling the extraction. This requires maturity and prayerful preparation on my part. If I think my character defect goes too deep or is too big for God to remove, then I know I'm limiting God. He is bigger than any character defect or any problem I might think I have. And he has changed me for the better, but he has done it gently and slowly, not in the fast and furious way I do things.

STEP EIGHT. Made a list of all persons we had harmed, and became willing to make amends to them all.

*M*any people get spooked by this step. Frequently, we feel *we* were the ones who were harmed in situations. Sometimes these feelings are justifiable and cause us to delay our amends or refuse to do them altogether.

Again, it isn't necessary to overcomplicate things. For the most part, the list of people I had harmed came from my Fourth Step. They were on the resentment and sexual inventories. I wrote down their names and asked God to direct me on this issue.

Other names nagged at my conscience though—people who were not on my Fourth Step, but about whom I still felt twinges of guilt. I had let them down or disappointed them in some way. I wanted to correct those situations, so I added their names to my Eighth Step list.

Next, I took my list to my sponsor. She had heard my Fifth Step so she was familiar with the circumstances surrounding most of the people on my list. And, like most individuals who manage to stay sober for many years, she had made her amends.

We went over the list of names and categorized them into the ones that I was better off not contacting, since it might cause them harm, and the ones I would be willing to meet. In reviewing the list, it became clear I often assumed responsibility for people's reactions, when this wasn't my responsibility at all. We scratched off these names as well.

47

This editing process shortened the list considerably, but it was also important because my sponsor had a more objective viewpoint and more wisdom than I had at the time. She knew better than I when amends were needed and when they weren't. She told me I would know when it was time for me to seek out these people and make amends. Step Eight is truly that simple: make the list, show it to someone, then become willing to start making direct amends. Some people begin immediately; others wait a few months.

As with any step, I prayed that God would reveal to me any people I had forgotten. I wanted him to soften my heart and enable me to approach the individuals on my amends list with a forgiving spirit and good will. I didn't want to add insult to injury and mess up my amends. I also didn't want to approach them with a chip on my shoulder and a demeanor of let's-get-this-over-with. I prayed hard for the right attitude and awareness.

STEP NINE. **Made direct amends to such people wherever possible, except when to do so would injure them or others.**

*M*ake no mistake about it, this is a very difficult step. In almost every case, the people on my list had harmed me in some way. I could easily have used that as rationalization for not beginning Step Nine and making my amends. It took a great deal of soul-searching to see where I had harmed others or caused turmoil in their lives.

Similarly, during my first year in recovery, I watched other recovering addicts and alcoholics flatly refuse to make amends to the people on their list. These addicts eventually returned to drugs and alcohol. It became obvious to me that the benefits of working these steps, such as peace of mind and freedom from fear, do not come to a lasting fruition until we make some headway on our Ninth Step. Those factors alone were incentive enough for me to at least be willing to consider doing this step.

I started with my husband. When I was using drugs, it seemed like the first words out of my mouth every morning and the last words at night were, "I'm sorry." He'd heard me say it so often that the words had no meaning anymore. When I made my amends to Harry, and everyone thereafter, I used the words, "I regret," instead of "I'm sorry." I told him I regretted putting him through the turmoil of my addiction: constant crises, the life and death scenes at the hospitals; frantic phone calls to his office

49

where I pleaded with him to leave work and come home to take care of me.

I also told him how I regretted the financial strain I'd put on him and our entire family. We owed thousands of dollars in overdraft charges at the bank and at hospitals all over town. He had just opened his own advertising agency and the pressures of starting up a new business, coupled with the financial disaster at home, must have been enormous. I had a peculiar way of comforting myself by purchasing things; this habit increased our already sizable financial hardships.

I also regretted that I had forced him to relive the horror of his own mother's death, who, at my same age, died from drug overdose. Her life and mine paralleled eerily. The first time I ever saw Harry cry was when I was in treatment and he begged me not to die like his mother had. He had to relive the grief and loss when the doctors told him I would probably die with a needle in my arm. They recommended he start attending Al-Anon immediately.

There was no question about it; I caused a great deal of harm to my husband. Many friends told me it was a miracle he stayed with me. I made my direct amends to him, but there was another kind of amends I needed to make—a living amends. Saying I was sorry or that I regretted my actions wasn't enough. I needed to change my behavior.

Concerning finances, the only way for me to make financial restitution was to stop my compulsive spending. I didn't realize it for quite a while, but whenever Harry said we needed to watch our spending, or that things were a little tight, my first reaction was to reassure myself and combat fear by buying something. Odd as it sounds, this was a blind spot for me. Once I became aware of my abnormal behavior, I was able to divert myself into more constructive activities. I learned to stay out of shopping malls; I didn't carry any credit cards with me; I threw away catalogues as soon as they were brought in from the mailbox. Anytime I had to buy something, I would time my shopping trip so that I would have to leave quickly for someplace else. That way I wouldn't linger and get into what I called my buying trance.

As my addiction to drugs increased, so did my dependence on Harry. If the children got sick, I called him and asked what to do. I asked him what to make for dinner, what to wear, where to go, whom to know. Every friend I made, I passed by him for approval. Once while on drugs, I called him from a gas station to ask him how to put gas in my car. This had to stop, for his benefit as well as mine.

Free from drugs, I now had to break my addiction of calling Harry at every little glitch. When the children got sick, I forced myself to call the pediatrician and take care of things myself. One day I went out to get in my car, and the rear tire was flat. My first impulse was to call Harry, but instead, I called a nearby gas station and they sent someone to change the tire. I developed my own circle of friends, people in recovery who didn't even know Harry. They were interested in me for my own sake, not because of whom I was married to. Harry's personality is very powerful and outgoing; I'm more reserved and introverted. Over the years I had learned to hide behind him, let people be dazzled by Harry and sooner or later they'd notice me. That pattern had to stop. I couldn't hide behind Harry or drugs or eccentricity anymore. I prayed for the courage to not be afraid of people anymore.

This was not a fast and easy process. My fingers wanted to dial Harry's office a dozen times a day. But, gradually, I accumulated other phone numbers, mostly of friends I could call when I was overwhelmed or confused. Others were service people: an honest plumber who didn't cheat me, repairmen who would come when I called, a pediatrician who trusted my judgment. Each time I made it over one of these hurdles without involving Harry, I felt exhilarated. I was doing it on my own!

I started out trying to make living amends to Harry by not being so dependent on him. And the result was that I benefited immensely. Little by little, I developed more confidence in myself. I went back to college and completed my degree in English literature. Sometimes I would even speak up in class. After graduation, I worked as an English teacher and won the respect of other teachers I knew. From this I learned these amends are not for the benefit of the other people. My living amends continue to benefit me in ways I never dreamed possible.

At ages four and six, my sons were too young to make direct amends to, but I implemented living amends as soon as I walked in my house after treatment. I cooked the foods they liked, instead of what was easiest; I helped them with their homework and listened to their rambling tales of what happened that day at school. It took a few months, but eventually, they trusted that I would remember conversations and important events. I wasn't stretched out on the couch anymore; I was up and moving around. I was a well mom, not a sick one. In short, I was a clean and sober mom.

As soon as I could gather the courage, I started attending their soccer games and other sporting events. At first, I sat far away from the parents in the stands. The yelling shattered my nerves and if someone tried to start a conversation with me, I wanted to run back to my car. But, season by season, I moved closer to the crowd, and today I can sit with the rest of the parents. Their cheering doesn't bother me and many of the other moms are now among my closest friends.

My amends to my children will continue for the rest of my life. Like all my amends, the rewards to me far outweigh the benefits my children might receive. Just this year, I've begun sharing bits of my story of drug addiction with them. They're teenagers now, and their grasp of the subject of addiction is remarkable. I can only hope that my struggle with drugs might prevent them from having to walk that path to hell. But if they do take it, they know where they can go for help.

The remainder of my amends were direct verbal amends. Not one of them was easy. The first amend that comes to mind was to my English professor and advisor. He went out of his way on several occasions to help me during my initial pursuit of an English degree and we developed a wonderful friendship over the years. But when the drugs got a firm hold on me, I blew up at him after class for the grade his assistant gave me on an exam. I was incensed that he would let a teacher's assistant grade my work! Didn't he know I was special?

A year or so later, I called and made an appointment to meet with him and make my amends. In the back of my mind, I thought he'd probably forgotten the incident in his classroom, and this would be a breeze. Well, he hadn't forgotten. He brought it up immediately, and I could tell his feelings were still hurt. This was an amends which definitely needed to be made, and after I was finished, he said that he was glad that I was back to being the real Melissa; the one he'd known before the drugs.

Amends to my parents were difficult, but necessary. They, too, voiced relief that I was getting help. It's easy to catalogue the wrongs inflicted on us by parents, even the best of them. But I had to reconcile with myself that I caused turmoil in their lives on many occasions, and that these amends were for me as well as for them. I was trying to stay clean, and if making amends to my parents was a hurdle I had to climb over on the path of recovery, then so be it.

There was one woman whom I swore I would never make amends to; she was a former employer. My second sober Christmas, I ran into her beside a sweater rack while I was shopping for my husband's gift. She appeared to be as stunned as I when we both reached for the same sweater and met one another's eyes. There she was, right in my face.

The opportunity presented itself; I needed to make amends to her. The Ninth Step says we made direct amends "wherever possible." To me, it was apparent this was one of those "wherever possible" times. This wasn't according to my timetable, but God's timing is always perfect and I couldn't pretend to ignore it. Reluctantly, we both went up to a cafe in the mall, and over a cup of tea I told her I regretted my behavior when I worked for her. Like my professor, she too had a good memory. I let her enumerate some of the insulting things I had done so many years earlier. Digging my fingernails into my palms, I resisted the temptation to tell her how difficult she had been to work for; then I reiterated my sincere regrets for my own immature behavior.

I fought the urge to bolt after making amends. I could tell something was still on her mind. Looking down at her tea, she told me she was battling cancer. Her breast and bladder had been removed; she'd given up on chemotherapy. She lived out in the country, far removed from her fashion industry friends, and her daughter had moved to another state. I sensed a vulnerability in her that day which was almost palpable.

Later that week, she invited me to her home for lunch, but I never felt comfortable. Our worlds were far apart now, and I think we both realized that the friendship had come to a graceful ending. I was glad I had made amends, but it was not necessary to resurrect the relationship. We kindly went our separate ways, and my side of the street was clean. That was what mattered to me.

In one other instance, I stated flat out that I would never make amends to a former girlfriend I made in early recovery. Her behavior became increasingly irritating so I did what I always did: abandoned the relationship. Three years had passed since I'd seen her and as far as I was concerned, she was totally in the wrong; I owed her nothing. One afternoon I boldly restated my refusal on this matter to a group of friends at lunch. This was one Ninth Step I was never going to make! And, look, it had been three years and I wasn't using drugs. So it must be okay...

A few minutes after I returned home that afternoon, she stepped up onto my front porch and rang the doorbell. I wanted to throw my hands up in the air and laugh at God's sense of humor! Instead, I let her in and calmly made my amends to her; after all, I knew that was why she was at my house. Likewise, she told me of her regrets in her own behavior. While our mutual apologies unfolded, I, for the first time, began to see where I had been dishonest with her. During our friendship, if she insisted on being included in my plans or made jokes at my expense, I never told her how much it bothered me. Instead, I seethed silently. As usual, I failed to state my own needs in that relationship and that failure on my part had a lot to do with the demise of the friendship.

We parted friends, spoke briefly on the phone a few times after that, but I don't think either one of us had the urge to resume the friendship. Making amends created a comfortable closure which allowed me a freedom to feel at ease whenever I saw this woman again. I wouldn't have to avoid her at parties or awkwardly fumble to make conversation in the grocery store. I could look her in the eye and feel right with myself. But we didn't have to be best friends again.

The most practical benefit of making amends comes at night. Prior to my amends, both of those women got a lot of free rent space in my head. Sometimes, I tossed and turned in bed and replayed the ways they had mistreated me. I concocted conversations where I would chew them out and let them know just what I, and everybody else, thought of them. I would awaken my husband and solicit his sympathy, forcing him, time and again, to reassure me I was not in the wrong. Those hours were wasted energy.

After I made the unwitting amends to them, I stopped lying awake at night thinking about them. I slept instead. The resentments vanished. As I write this, I can't recall what it was either of those two women did in particular to make me so angry. That's a far cry from the way it was originally: they had, at separate times in my life, generated tremendous indignation. Now the thought of them remains completely neutral. That's a miracle.

To sum up the Ninth Step, never say never. The two times I've refused to make amends, the person has appeared in my path and making amends was inescapable. The purpose of the Ninth Step is to clean up my side of the street so I can rest comfortably knowing my conscience is clear. Making amends lets me walk away knowing I've done the best I could to correct my part in the relationship, and I've learned to avoid making those same mistakes in other friendships.

Guilt, resentment, hate, fear: these are sentiments that tormented my soul for too long, and ultimately demanded medication. Too often, that form of treatment was drugs. The comforting effects of making amends enables me to go through my days without anesthetizing myself.

Today, I don't have to deaden the pangs of guilt or waves of hatred. Those old wounds were healed by exposing them to the light and doing the right thing: making amends. After I took the action, God did the rest. He restored my family relationships, and breathed new life into my marriage which staggered under the weight of old hurts and resentments. He took the venom out of stings from broken friendships and let me see the ways in which I can be a better, more honest friend in the future. I have found that if I do the footwork, God always performs a miracle which is beyond anything I could have imagined.

STEP TEN. **Continued to take personal inventory and when we were wrong promptly admitted it.**

Steps Ten, Eleven and Twelve are frequently referred to as the maintenance steps. After I completed the first nine steps, I put to rest the shame and resentments that, in large part, made up the wreckage of my past. Step Ten helps me stay on the right path, day to day. Worked on a daily or weekly basis, it prevents me from forming new resentments or developing self-destructive behaviors which always seem to appear out of nowhere.

This year at Easter, a friend gave me a beautiful blooming tropical plant. Each week, I put it in the kitchen sink and trim off the withered blooms and yellow leaves. Then I give it a big drink of water from the kitchen faucet. The plant continues to thrive and produce flowers because I take a few minutes to remove the dead foliage which, if left unattended, deprive it of needed nutrients and detract from its appearance.

Tending this plant closely parallels the Tenth Step. Every so often, I run a quick inventory of myself and see if I'm nursing any resentment, or if a certain fear is taking control of my life. This applies to obsessions as well. If I'm spending too much time thinking about something or someone, before I know it I'm obsessing on them. Obsession, resentments or fear are like the deadwood that saps me of my energy and prevents me from being of service to anyone.

When I take the inventory and find a sore spot, I usually begin by discussing it with my sponsor who can offer a more coolheaded approach to the subject. Sometimes, just talking about it takes the power out of a problem, particularly obsessions. Usually, we both end up by laughing about the entire matter. Then it's easily put aside. Without my being aware of it, I've turned the matter over to God, I've surrendered it. And until I've made this surrender, I will continue to suffer.

But there are times when a frank discussion isn't enough. I continue to harbor the resentment or give in to fears. At that point, I have to pick up my pen and write out a brief inventory about that particular problem. If it's a resentment, I go back to the format I used on Step Four. I write about what caused the resentment, what its effects are and what my part is in the problem. Then I read it to my sponsor or someone else who has worked the steps. They listen, then they give their feedback.

Taking the inventory, though, is only half of the Tenth Step. The second part of Step Ten says: "...when we were wrong promptly admitted it." I remember my first encounter with this step. I had worked my Nine Steps and felt like a new person. I'd been off drugs for close to a year and tried with all my might to say and do the right things. Then, one day, I was talking on the phone to my mother and a lie just popped out of my mouth. It was a harmless one—flattering to her, in fact. But it was a lie, nonetheless.

It tugged at my conscience the entire afternoon, so I thought I'd admit it to someone. I decided I'd take the easy way out; I would call my husband and admit to *him* that I lied to my mother. I was sure he'd think it was a minor offense. Then I'd be done with it. But his response was nothing like what I expected. He laughed suspiciously and reminded me that when I was wrong, I had to *promptly* admit it. In this case, admitting it to him meant nothing. I needed to promptly admit it to my mother!

I was incredulous. How could he have such a strenuous interpretation of this step, I wondered. So I called a woman whose opinion I respect immensely and asked her if Harry was right. He was. Reluctantly, I called my mother and sheepishly admitted that I had lied during our earlier phone conversation. I promptly made the amends and told her I regretted the lie.

She accepted my amends with extraordinary courtesy, and told me she'd done the same thing many times. At that moment, I learned from my mother how to graciously accept amends, and I began to break my insidious habit of lying. After that, if I slipped up and told a lie, I *promptly* backtracked and admitted it to the person to whom I had lied. This is a surefire way to break any habit. And lying is more than a habit for a drug addict, it's second nature. Lying is part of what I call my "junkie behavior" and I want to do away with as many of those behaviors as possible.

Step Ten is essential to the preservation of any marriage. My relationship with Harry certainly is helped by frequently working Step Ten. For one thing, I am more aware of my behaviors; if I'm feeling angry, I do a quick spot-check inventory on myself and make sure I don't say something I'll regret later. On more than one occasion, I've been upset with Harry in the morning, talk the issue out with a dispassionate friend, and by the time he comes home from work that night, I'll have worked through the entire problem without involving him at all. No name calling, no hysterics, no attacks. This, I'm sure, is a relief to him and it saves me from having to make amends.

But, it hasn't always been that easy. In my early sobriety, I would rage at Harry over the smallest infraction, real or imagined. I was sure he was trying to undermine me with our children, and I heard innuendo and criticism in every statement. My perceptions were distorted, my thinking processes were ravaged by drugs, and it took me almost a year to get beyond my hair trigger temper. Harry threatened to leave me if I didn't stop attacking him; he said the rages were too much for him to endure.

One of the ways in which I was able to drain off this rage was by writing about how I felt toward my parents. My sponsor, who has been by my side throughout recovery, walked me through this process. I discovered a tremendous reservoir of rage and listed every demeaning, frightening incident I could recall. Then my sponsor and I went over them one by one. She'd had a childhood similar to mine, and in many ways worse. So we could communicate easily about these articles without shame or fear of being discovered. It helped me to know that I was not the only one who'd experienced this level of anger and disgrace.

Once my rage was out in the open, most of it dissipated. I was able to see that my hostility wasn't hurting my parents; they were unaware of it. But it was injuring me and seriously jeopardizing my marriage. I saw that my parents raised me while they were fighting their own emotional battles with alcoholism. They couldn't have done their job of parenting any better. I had to forgive myself for acting like them at times. Once I forgave myself, I was able to forgive them.

All along, I thought my anger at Harry was justified. But my anger was misplaced. I realized he was not my enemy; I was. The rage diminished and so did the crippling remorse I always felt in its wake. Today I guard against rage as I would a lethal intruder. If I'm angry at someone or something, I keep that anger discreetly upon that one subject, and try not to let it generalize into other facets of my life, particularly toward Harry. I make sure I don't get too hungry or tired. These are always the precursors to problems. In addition, I've learned to avoid too much sugar. A donut for breakfast can turn me into a screaming lunatic by noon.

Routine applications of Step Ten prevent grudges, fears and obsessions from building up. A hatred that festers or an obsession that grows, distracts me from what I'm really supposed to be doing. This is information which I believe most mortals already possess. They watch their behavior, and admit it when they're wrong. But this was new and very awkward for me in the beginning. Over the years, I've had many opportunities to practice Step Ten, and now it comes naturally to me. Notice, I didn't say it comes easily.

Although it's difficult to admit it when I'm wrong, I've found it's essential in sustaining relationships and staying truthful with myself and others. Many of the relationships I enjoy today are several years old. In the past, that wasn't possible. I'd stay friends with someone until they hurt my feelings; then it would be over. Due to Step Ten, my friendships stay honest, and above all, kind. I speak up when I feel hurt, and I admit it when I've said or done something harmful to someone else. Likewise, I hold my tongue when I feel the urge to criticize or chastise. Criticism never changed me; why would I think it could change anyone else? Only love and kindness changed me. And that, I discovered, at forty years old, is how friends stay friends and wives stay lovers.

STEP ELEVEN. Sought through prayer and meditation to improve our conscious contact with God *as we understood Him,* praying only for knowledge of His will for us and the power to carry that out.

I started working Step Eleven by dropping to my knees every morning and saying a quick prayer for God to keep me off drugs and to take care of my children. Then at night, before going to sleep, Harry and I held hands and each said a brief prayer aloud, thanking God for the day and for keeping me sober. After a couple of years, I desired something more; I longed for a deeper relationship with God. I desired the type of faith I read about and peace of mind that flows from a life without fear. More than anything else, I wanted emotional balance.

Thoughts of suicide still tormented my thinking. Depressions caused me to dip too low and sometimes I would go on emotional binges that left me exhausted. I craved the balance I saw in the lives of other people in recovery. The common thread in their lives was that they meditated. Some practiced yoga breathing techniques; others read the St. Francis prayer and meditated on that for several minutes each day. A few simply quieted their minds and thought about God each morning before they began their day.

My spiritual journey has led me down many paths. I soon discovered there was no right or wrong way to meditate. All I had to do was make a feeble attempt to contact

God and he would do the rest. After reading stacks of books and asking dozens of questions, I finally embarked on my own form of meditation.

Praise is the key I use at the beginning of my prayer and meditation to unlock the door to God. Instead of beseeching him to help me with this or that, I thank him for the many wondrous blessings he has restored in my life. For one thing, he's given me back my life; my children are healthy and my marriage is a source of joy and peace. The litany of things for which I am grateful is long most days. Other days, when I'm not feeling so grateful, I simply thank him for the sunlight filtering through my bedroom window or the physical ability to kneel beside my bed.

After my prayers, I sit in a comfortable chair in my bedroom and read a passage from one of my daily meditation books. Several books for people in recovery are available with daily meditations, and I frequently use these. But my favorite standby is a small book called *God Calling*. Each date has its own spiritual message and I get excellent direction early in the day from these inspirational passages.

When I finish the reading for that date, I close my eyes. If my mind is particularly jittery and I'm unable to quiet my thoughts, I borrow from the Yoga techniques, and very slowly breathe in through my nose and exhale through my mouth. I do this about three or four times. Then, I try to focus my thoughts on the meditation passage I have just read. After a few minutes, my mind relaxes, tension dissipates. And sometimes I don't think of anything at all. When thoughts come, I quietly repeat to myself, "Come Holy Spirit, fill my heart and thoughts." I do this for as long as twenty minutes, or as short as five minutes, depending on my schedule.

Another technique I borrowed is from the transcendental meditation followers. My younger brother was an avid believer in this method for several years and taught me how to use a mantra to calm my mind. Instead of using the mantra he gave me, though, I use the name Jesus. I say His name over and over in my mind. This has an overall calming effect and usually works when nothing else will.

After my period of meditation, I open my eyes and think about my day. I try to avoid filling up my day with too many errands and rat race activities. I purposefully leave several hours open for God to do with me as he pleases. There is usually some errand for him which needs to be run. For example today, around noon, I had just settled myself comfortably on a raft in my pool. The radio was playing thirty minutes of commercial-free music and I thought this would be a perfect time to work on my tan.

But God had something else in mind. Just as I felt comfortable, I got a phone call that a good friend collapsed from a heart attack and had to be rushed by ambulance to a nearby hospital. Several people were on their way to be with him, but they wanted to let me know before they left for the hospital. I placed the phone back on the edge of the pool and deliberated about what I should do. Other people would be there, I thought as I laid back on the raft. After all, I deserved some time for myself; I'd been shuttling kids all summer. As I drifted into the center of the pool, the truth came loud and clear. I had to go to my friend. Sometimes, what I perceive as an interruption is really what God would have me do.

Grumbling at God, I dragged myself and my raft out of the pool and showered. On the way to the hospital, I prepared the speech I was going to give my friend for his smoking and terrible eating habits. When I arrived, I was surprised to see that no one else was there. Dan was in bad shape. Panting like a wounded animal, he laid helplessly on the gurney. Tubes were inserted in his nose and arms and the heart monitor over his head loudly spewed out a strip of paper imprinted with dangerously irregular heart patterns. My prepared speech completely left my mind, and was miraculously replaced with compassion, God's compassion.

When Dan saw me he weakly squeezed my hand and told me through gasps of air how relieved he was that I was there. With terror in his eyes, he pleaded with me to stay. I put my hand over his and told him to be calm and breathe slowly through his nose. I don't know why I told him to do that. He closed his mouth, breathed slowly and his heart rate immediately stabilized. The frustration I had felt earlier vanished from my thoughts. The only thing I thought of was my concern for his life and of all the people who depended on him for love and support. These were God's thoughts, not mine.

Finally, other people started arriving for him. The nurses got irritated with the growing crowd and I knew it was time to leave; I was no longer of any service. So I drove home and thanked God for giving me a lifestyle which allows me to run his errands. I offered up my day to him that morning and he filled the time usefully. This was God's will for me today. I have no idea what it will be tomorrow.

When I sit in the morning and think about my day, I ask God to direct my thinking as well as my actions. Dishonesty, self-pity and self-seeking are culprits that I ask him to remove from my mind. I want to go out into the world with purified thoughts and an open heart. I avoid heated arguments and controversial situations. If I become frustrated with traffic or daily life, I try to pause and take time to withdraw from the chaos for brief meditative retreats.

Emotional balance has been one of the many gifts of this prayerful discipline. The last killer depression I suffered was over three years ago. I avoid getting too high or too low. Staying level is a blessing I never thought possible without chemicals. But I try to begin every day by surrendering it to the will of God. My will for myself is not always a safe one. By asking God to direct my day, I feel as if I'm fulfilling my purpose in this life. God is never far from my thoughts and I rarely feel alone.

After following this regime, which takes far less time to do than to write about, I go on about my business. I want to do God's will and I've often struggled to know what that is. After years of study and prayer, I've discovered what God's will is *not.* It is not God's will if I have to lie about some facet of what I'm doing. It is not God's will if it only benefits me. And it's never God's will if someone will be hurt by what I'm saying or doing. That's all I know right now about God's will.

Over the past few years, addiction has been described by some great authors and psychiatrists as a spiritual yearning. An addict will satisfy that yearning with drugs. Some people use food or shopping or gambling or even sex to fill that void. When we quit using these things, we're left with the void and we frantically look for a quick fix. We might find that fix in compulsive behaviors which have the look and feel of positive addictions: overwork, excessive exercising or dieting, high-drama relationships, antidepressants, cult-like religions. What harm could these do? They offer us some relief and they give definition to our lives. They aren't hurting anybody, right?

It has been my experience that daily prayer and meditation satisfies that spiritual yearning in my soul. It's not a quick fix. For some, the rewards are immediate, but for me it took almost a year for the emotional balance to take hold. I was no longer flying from one end of the emotional spectrum to the other, suicide thoughts didn't consume me, fears didn't control me. I learned that no human power could relieve my drug addiction. No one person, man or woman has that much power. It takes dozens of people in my recovery meetings telling me how they cope with their own problems to teach me how to cope with mine. And it takes prayer and meditation for me to remain sane and sober without mind-altering chemicals.

STEP TWELVE. **Having had a spiritual awakening as the result of these steps, we tried to carry this message to alcoholics and addicts, and to practice these principles in all our affairs.**

*M*y initial reaction to this step was, forget it! I took care of my alcoholic mother and I wasn't about to go through that again. Throughout my adult life, I had made a point to avoid drunks. Their voices, their smells and belligerence all brought back grim memories. Some other poor fool could go to their aid. I'd had enough. I clung stubbornly to this refusal until one day at a meeting, I heard a statement that seared my heart: "You can't keep this gift if you don't give it away." The gift they were referring to was sobriety.

A few weeks after I heard this, a young woman close to my age and with two children the same ages as mine asked me to help her stop using drugs. While she tearfully described her struggle with crack, I immediately identified with her pain. She was trying desperately to be a good mother and wife, but the drugs had taken her over so completely she was a physical and mental wreck. Her marriage was on its last legs and her young children were practically raising themselves.

This woman's anguish ignited something in me. I found myself leaning close to her, telling her about my walk through addiction, pointing out the parallels in our lives. I assured her she could have a life that wasn't owned by drugs. She never had to feel this bad again. In short, I was doing the same thing for her that had been done for me and hundreds like me over the past sixty years. I was working the Twelfth Step, in spite of myself. This was the beginning of my spiritual awakening; I lost sight of myself; my concern for another outweighed all thoughts of my own fear-centered convictions.

This scene has been repeated for me on countless occasions. I've sat with dazed housewives who refuse to stop taking their tranquilizers and pain pills, and I've talked with wild-eyed hookers who couldn't leave the cocaine alone. I've watched nurses lose their licenses because they wrote out illegal prescriptions for themselves; I've known two women who have lost their children to government agencies because drugs were more important than their kids. But there have been a few addicts I've encountered who have stayed with the program and were willing to work the Twelve Steps. Now their lives are as normal as anyone else's; they are contributing members of society, and they have their dignity. Unfortunately, this program is not for those who need it; it's for those who want it. Millions of people need to sober up, but they simply don't want to. The prospects of life without drugs is too terrifying for them.

Yesterday a relative called me. She and her husband live an idyllic existence with their three young children in a beautiful resort village. He makes an excellent living; she volunteers at her daughters' schools and various other endeavors. They ski, ice skate, play golf, go to church on Sundays. They're leaders in their community, a family to be admired. But their lives are slowly and secretly being destroyed by alcoholism.

He doesn't drink every day like his parents did, and because of that he is sure he's not an alcoholic. In his opinion, he doesn't need help. He believes he can control

it on his own. I cannot help him, but I can love him. When
he asks, I tell him my experiences, but he doesn't hear the
similarities, only the differences. I pray someone else will
come along who can help him. Presently, all I can do is
direct his wife to Al-Anon. Then I have to turn them both
over to God. He needs the program, but he doesn't want
it. Yet.

Coincidentally, at church this Sunday, a visiting minister
gave a sermon on addiction. I sat dumbfounded as she
described the alcoholic death of her thirty-five-year-old
brother in New York City. She said his apartment was
across the street from an Episcopal church that had over
ten AA and NA meetings per week. Her brother could
never bring himself to cross that street to ask for help.
Addiction, she said, is a disease of isolation, and it feeds
on self-pity.

Obviously, the Twelfth Step can be tricky with family
members. A minister can help total strangers get into
recovery, but neither she nor I can help our family members to stop drinking. I've quit asking why. The people
who guided me into sobriety were strangers. I desperately
wanted their help because I had totally lost faith in my own
ideas. I had no more answers. I gladly followed the instruc-
tions of the women I met who had learned how to get
through their days without drugs. And I followed them
with blind faith. I surrendered my own will. As with all
spiritual awakenings, a surrender is necessary before God
can come in and straighten the inner twists and torments
of our souls.

My spiritual awakening didn't come in the form of a
burning bush or life-changing vision. It is a daily process
which takes place, often without my even knowing it.
Suddenly, I'm aware that I intuitively know how to handle
things that formerly baffled me. I realize with wonder that
I've gone several years without using drugs or alcohol. I

now have people in my life whereas I formerly avoided human contact at all cost. Loneliness and isolation are replaced by a group of friends and freedom from the conviction that I need drugs in order to live. Very simply, I can open the blinds on my windows every morning and leave the house without feeling for the reassuring touch of Valium and painkillers in my pockets.

One final example of how the Twelve Steps have changed my life comes to mind due to a recent event with one of my sons. Several years ago, when I was in the final stages of drug addiction, my five-year-old son came running into the house with blood streaming down his face. A neighbor boy had thrown a rock at Sage and the stone made about an inch-long incision along his hairline.

I had taken more pills than I could count by that hour in the day, and I was terrified at the prospect of driving to a chaotic hospital emergency room and dealing with medical people. The situation baffled me. So I caved into my fears and clumsily taped the wound shut myself. I rationalized that the cut wasn't deep enough for stitches; tape would suffice. The wound healed, but a fairly wide scar still shows now, nine years later. It isn't disfiguring, but it's there, nonetheless. If I had been in my right mind, I would have taken him to the emergency room, and the scar wouldn't be noticeable today.

In contrast, a few days ago I was working on this book at my computer when the phone rang. It was the lifeguard at our neighborhood country club. She told me that my youngest son had done a backflip on the diving board and injured his head. Did I live close by or should she call an ambulance? I made it to the club in three minutes. I had horror-filled thoughts during those three minutes, sure that my athletic thirteen-year-old son was paralyzed for life. But when I got there, he was sitting on a stool with a bloody wad of napkins on his head. I gathered him and his belongings together and quickly drove to the emergency room. His wound was cleaned and sewn together and he won't have a scar on his head like his older brother has.

This time I was not baffled. I knew what to do and I efficiently moved through the tasks. The thought of the emergency room or facing doctors and nurses didn't terrify me. Nothing in fact terrified me, except the prospect of what could have happened. I've thanked God several times for taking care of my child and protecting him from something much worse than a cut on the head. And I thanked him for giving me the sanity to handle the situation like a normal, sober mother would.

As a result of working these Twelve Steps, I've had a spiritual awakening. I've developed a relationship and a closeness with God. He frequently gives me the poise and intelligence to handle situations that I couldn't cope with previously. Other times, my best effort is reduced to a fearful bumbling attempt to get through whatever the crisis is. No one says we have to be graceful at this. I'm often afraid. But I heard somewhere that courage is fear that has said its prayers; and that I most assuredly have done.

Also, as instructed in the Twelfth Step, I've tried to carry this message to other drug addicts. Several have worked the steps just as I did and received benefits too numerous to count. Their lives, like mine, are restored beyond anything we could have hoped for. And these same women help other addicts in their work places, in their neighborhoods and communities. When any of us stop helping other addicts and get caught up in our own lives, the results are always the same: depression, loneliness and isolation. The antidote for this despair feels like the least appealing, but it is the most effective: help another addict. This always works at lifting a depression or breaking an obsession. And it keeps me sober.

None of us could have gotten to the places we are today

without the help of God and of one another. We don't pat ourselves on the back and say look how great I'm doing. Instead, we unreservedly give full credit where it belongs, to the grace of God and to the patient kindness of other addicts who went before us. The number of hours that recovering addicts spent with me, the free spiritual guidance and wisdom that I've received from these courageous people is something I will never be able to repay. They did for me what I could not do for myself. And I firmly believe that God works through each and every one of us. We are his hands and feet and sometimes his voice; he wants us to take care of each other.

My husband came home from church about a year ago and eagerly retold a powerful sermon he had heard that morning. It seems the final voice recordings of the failed Challenger mission were released, but hadn't been publicized. Our minister had access to the recordings and was so moved by what she heard that she created her sermon around it. After the doomed rocket ship's occupants realized their horrible fate, the last words on the tape were said by a young school teacher. She said to the person strapped in beside her, "Please, hold my hand."

The touching simplicity of this action perfectly symbolizes the Twelve Steps to me. We addicts know full well we're dying. But, if we're lucky, before we crash we find someone's hand to hold onto. Too many of us die horrible deaths alone in hospital beds, gutters, mansions, and missions. If we make that last excruciating effort to reach out our hand for human contact, we can get a second chance at life. We don't ever have to suffer alone anymore.

Magazines, talk shows and movies are teeming with stories of addicts who wouldn't get help. Every day a judge's gavel hammers out the end for another family shattered by addiction. Before I finish writing this paragraph, someone will die in my city from addiction. The death certificate may list it as cirrhosis, liver failure, gunshot wounds, car accident, suicide, carbon monoxide inhalation, heart attack, prescription complications. But the real reason is addiction, plain and simple.

If you are married to an addict, start by getting help for yourself. This isn't just the addict's problem, it's your problem too. Al-Anon offers the same Twelve Steps that I've listed here. You'll find people who have walked in your shoes and can share their experience, strength and hope with you. You'll learn new ways of living with addiction which enable you to enjoy life in spite of your partner's disease. And the current of your own recovery may sweep the addict along into these healing waters as well.

Too often, the husbands and wives of addicts get momentary illusions of reprieve. Recently, the wife of an addict told me her husband had his driver's license revoked for several months, so she didn't feel it was necessary for him to attend AA. She surmised that since she was driving him everywhere, she would always know where he was. Therefore, he wouldn't drink! To me, this rationale would be amusing if it weren't so lethal. They usually mean well, but frequently husbands and wives can actually kill their addict spouse out of ignorance, embarrassment or expediency.

Today a handsome, newly-recovering cocaine addict told me he is glad his wife hasn't sought out recovery in Al-Anon. He laughingly confided that his wife still thinks the reason he became addicted to drugs was her. As long as she'll take on the guilt for his problems, I suppose he'll let her.

Recovery is never convenient. Twelve Step meetings, writing out the steps, working with others, prayer and meditation, all these things take time. I didn't seem to mind the fact that I lost days, weeks, even years to my addiction. I would gladly spend hours and hundreds of dollars going to a doctor to get a prescription, then I bought the pills with money that was intended to buy groceries. I spent the better part of each day getting, taking, then sleeping off the drugs. Yet, when I was told that I had to take an hour out of my day to attend recovery meetings, I bristled and said that I was too busy.

But I was willing to try it, if only for one day. Then, the next day and the next. I was so amazed that I was able to put a twenty-four hour period together without drugs. I kept doing what I was supposed to do and the going got a little easier with each passing day. I expected loneliness and panic to settle in like they had so many times before recovery. But they didn't. The fellowship of other recovering addicts kept me buoyed up; my head was always above water in spite of how hard I struggled. I sensed for the first time in my life that others understood me. And my family quickly accepted that my recovery was a daily appointment I had to keep.

My husband began his recovery at the same time I did. He has never lost sight of the fact that I live with a death sentence over my head. If I stop going to meetings and working my steps, I will return to drugs. And that means sure death—or worse, a living death locked in some mental ward. The greatest gift I can give to my children is to be a sober mother. For my husband, I am a sane wife. I don't depend on him to fix me anymore. No single human power can relieve me of my addiction. It takes rooms full of people and a daily conscious contact with God for that to happen.

It amazes me that so often families of addicts think, if only he or she would get sober, then everything will be all right. If that were true, the Twelve Steps wouldn't be necessary. But a drug addict without drugs is a very uncomfortable, and often unpleasant person. Descriptions like irritable, impatient and edgy frequently apply.

That's where the Twelve Steps come in. The discomfort of living without drugs is gradually removed by working the steps. Each one offers more relief. By the time I finished the steps, I realized I could laugh again. It felt strange at first, but it was there. Loneliness was a distant memory and the thought of taking drugs was just that, a thought. I didn't have to act on it.

Every year I meet with a small group of women and we study the Twelve Steps in depth. Over the course of twelve weeks, we read and discuss every aspect of each step and how it applies to our own lives. Pain comes up, revelations occur, tears are shed, but the process heals any emotional wounds we've incurred over the previous year. Each time I do this, I learn something new about each of the Twelve Steps and I develop a deeper appreciation of God's infinite love and forgiveness.

Healing always hurts. I remember after having a baby that I felt like I had sat on a blender with the setting at puree. But I healed. And while I healed, I hurt. After my son cut his head on the diving board, his head was tender and he winced when we applied the medicine. After it healed he didn't hurt anymore. Anyone who's had an operation knows the worst part is after surgery; the incision hurts and the healing process is painstakingly slow.

Emotional healing is painful too. It often involves uncovering ancient anger and malignant memories. Emotional restoration involves self-examination and sometimes suffering great shame. It takes courage and humility to participate in this healing process. An addict can stop the process at any time by picking up a drink or a drug. But if we persevere and enlist the support of others who have made the same spiritual journey, we will wake up one day without terror.

I've discovered these emotional wounds are healed when I am able to use them redemptively. If I share an experience with someone who is suffering, and I use that occurrence to help guide them through their own pain, the memory is redeemed. The experience is purified and put to good use. Oftentimes, some of our most shameful experiences can be purified and healed in this manner.

It isn't my desire to take anyone's pain away from them. I'm out of the business of pain avoidance. But I can share whatever similar experiences I might have with them to offer a glimmer of hope, as was done for me when I confronted the pain of my own addiction. With the help of these steps, complete recovery in every aspect of life is possible.

My Name Is

HARRY

Prologue

A couple of things first. Don't expect Melissa's prologue to be the same as mine. Or her First Step. Or anything. That's the deal about recovery. It doesn't happen in sync. In fact, it can't. You go at your rate, your partner goes at hers. The best you can hope for is that she's in there trying, that she's sober, that she's calling her sponsor, going to meetings, not using. That's it. Hope for anything more and you're going to be disappointed. Well, not just disappointed, but destroyed. Because she might not make it.

So the first thing you learn in recovery is that it's your recovery you're dealing with, not hers. Which, if you have any control issues at all, is a difficult thing to grasp.

I'm going over this now so you don't read her Step One, then my Step One, then say, "Well these two people lived on different planets." Because yes, we did. And when you're in the early stages of recovery, you have to live on different planets. No matter how much you love her, you cannot help her get better. She cannot help you get better. You can meet in the kitchen every now and then and hug each other and encourage each other. But the fact is, to come together, you have to grow apart. As in *grow* apart. As in improve. Only then can you grow together. It's weird. I know. I've lived through it.

I adore my wife. I've been madly in love with her since we first met at Neiman-Marcus over twenty years ago. She is still the sexiest woman I've ever met. We've always laughed a lot. We've always clung to each other, encouraged each other, taken care of each other. I am reassured by her touch. Her voice on the phone can lift me up.

But somehow, this very honest, open love I had for her turned obsessive and destructive. I understand today what happened: I was afraid she was going to die. Long before she took her first pill.

In an effort to keep her from dying, I became my wife's pusher. I was also her biggest critic, her parent, her protector, in many ways her god. None of which, of course, has anything to do with a healthy marriage.

My goal was to make sure she—and later my children—never felt pain, because pain leads to death. Such a goal can only cause a more incredible, destructive pain, but that was my goal. I was terrified they would feel pain. So I did everything in my power to keep her and them from hurting. If she and a neighbor were having a fight, instead of comforting her, I would get mad that she even had a conversation with that person. If she was scared of going someplace alone, I would go with her. If she hated her job, I wept. If she felt alone, I would race home. I encouraged her to join tennis clubs, craft clubs, women's groups, all of which she hated. But I didn't want her to suffer the pain of loneliness. If she had to have something, I would find a way to buy it. If she cried, I comforted her.

If she had a headache, I would give her a pill.

In the beginning of our marriage, it was simply Excedrin. But for a three-year period, it became Valium, Vicodan, Vistaril, Equegisic, Restoril—or if things got really bad, I would take her to the hospital for a shot of Demerol. I never really considered the fact that she might be taking too many drugs until the very end. Addiction to prescription pills is so insidious, because the husband or wife or parent may not know for years what is actually happening. If I had come home and Melissa had been passed out on the couch with a bottle of vodka between her legs, I would have been enraged.

But when you come home and your wife is passed out on the couch from the Valium she took for her headache, well that made perfect sense to me. In fact, I would often rush to the drugstore to buy more Valium or whatever pain pill the doctor had prescribed, if she was running low. I never thought it odd that Melissa never ran out of pills; she would merely run low. And I thought everyone had a $700 monthly drugstore bill.

"How could you be so blind?" you might ask. It was simple. The thought of Melissa being in pain was terrifying to me. And her headaches caused her an ungodly amount of pain: she would be throwing up, crying, shaking. It wouldn't just break my heart, it would rip my soul. I would have given her a hundred Valium if I thought they could stop the pain.

Melissa also tried hard to be a perfect mother and wife. It wasn't as if all she did was take pills. We still laughed. We still hugged. We still cared deeply for each other. Our two boys were regularly fed, seemingly happy and well adjusted. They were trained to take a lot of naps, of course, since their mother faithfully passed out every day after lunch, but young children needed a lot of sleep, which also made perfect sense to me. We took vacations. And I worried a lot about her headaches.

Over time, her pills became a thing like eating breakfast. We just didn't think about it. Her headaches would come in flurries, so some nights we went out and some nights we didn't. Some nights she would have to go to bed early, some nights she wouldn't. A day didn't pass when she didn't take four or five Valiums just to be on the safe side, but again, it seemed normal to me. No one thought she had a problem, least of all me.

I frankly was concerned she might have a headache

without her pills nearby. The thought of that was too awful to contemplate. I had seen her throw up. I held her when she was sobbing from the pain. I would gladly race to an all-night drugstore, or take her to the hospital or stay up all night with her, anything to help take away the pain. Her mother actually worried out loud about the pills one time, and I exasperatedly told her, "Melissa doesn't have a pill problem. She has a headache problem."

I couldn't see that pills were a problem—we led an ideal life. We had two beautiful boys, a dream home, a Mercedes; I worked for a great company, Melissa was head of the women's group at church, I coached two soccer teams and taught Sunday School. We took trips to Hawaii. I brought Melissa along on many of my television shoots to places like San Francisco and Los Angeles for romantic weekends. Talent agents were falling over themselves to have our kids model for them. We had everything. Including headaches.

I had them too. Before Melissa developed hers, before she had prescriptions for countless different pain medications, I was hospitalized for two weeks with bizarre and crushing headaches so severe that doctors believed I had an aneurysm. Pools of blood had formed in different places around my head causing me literally to lose consciousness from the pain. To counteract it, I was being given Demerol shots every four hours, plus assorted pain medications, sedatives and other stuff. Basically I was stoned silly.

Melissa visited me every day, though between the pain and the drugs I don't remember a lot. But she would later say that one day as the pain was quite crippling, a nurse came in and injected me with Demerol, and as Melissa saw the needle going into my body, the liquid going in and my facial features relaxing at the same time, she was flushed with a feeling more intense than anything she's ever known before.

Six weeks later I was in Memphis visiting a client. I called home from the airport only to have my mother-in-law answer the phone and say, "Harry, everything's all right. But Melissa's head was killing her and she was throwing up from the pain. She went to see your doctor. She's having migraines."

I panicked. My wife was in pain. I *knew* the pain she was in. I prayed all the way home that God would give me her pain.

The next three years were, by any definition, insane. Not just because she took pills. But the more she hurt, the more I tried to keep her from hurting. As she was losing control, I was losing control. Somewhere along the line I decided, if I was the best husband and father in the world, she wouldn't be in pain anymore. Her headaches would go away.

So as her headaches became more frequent I would wake and feed the boys, take them to Mother's Day Out, drive to work, receive two or three desperate phone calls from my wife before noon, work out, leave work early to pick the boys up, go to the store, come home, play with the boys, deal with her headache, help make dinner, take one or both kids to soccer practice, go to some soccer board meeting, drive home—and collapse in bed.

On weekends I would go to the store, go to soccer games, keep the kids out of the house. And work in the yard maybe sixteen hours. (More about compulsions later.) And quite often, in the middle of the night, I'd take her to the hospital for a shot. We began arguing more. She threatened to leave many, many times, which was my greatest fear. I knew something was wrong, but I just couldn't nail it down.

I felt that I could never make her happy. I felt like she

was having headaches because of me, because of our middle class situation, because I didn't make enough money. I had no idea of the amount of drugs she was taking, but even if I had known, they were doctor-prescribed, so I couldn't have possibly questioned them. We might have lived this way another two or three years and she would have tragically and mysteriously died. I would have had no idea what happened or why God would do this to me.

But I got fired from my dream job. And immediately my life began to cave in on me.

Melissa later said that when I told her I had gotten fired, pain just ripped through her head. And basically never left. I immediately decided not to seek another job, but rather start my own company. Fortunately, I left with a small pension and a few days later became a founder of a creative boutique.

We started showing a profit within six weeks, but Melissa's headaches incredibly became worse. So bad, she couldn't get out of bed. She started calling her doctor asking for a hospital stay. The reason was simple—a hospital stay included regularly scheduled blasts of Demerol, all-in-all a pretty swell knockout shot that leaves you on the ceiling. But her doctor kept putting her off until after two weeks in bed and her umpteenth phone call, he relented and told her to come to Medical City.

A sigh of relief emanated from her body. Even though she had been bedridden two weeks, she lit up when her doctor told her she could go to the hospital. She had it in her mind she was going on a Demerol holiday. Melissa rose from the dead out of her bed, took a long bath, did her hair, her nails, her toenails. I, of course, was a blithering idiot, because I just wanted her to get rid of the pain and she was taking an hour and half just to get ready. She walked out of the bathroom looking like a million dollars— to go to the hospital. I didn't know at the time that she was planning on injections of Demerol for three days every four hours buffered by Valium and the like. Truly, a drug addict's dream vacation.

But an incredible thing happened, which is—that didn't happen.

The doctors (and there were plenty at the end) decided the Valium was the cause of her headaches, and put her on simple aspirin. Now an alert husband would have soon picked up the fact something was wrong because forty-eight hours later she was screaming at me over the phone about her doctors, and their aspirin, and she was going to rip their hearts out.

I was in a state of panic. Once again. Not because my wife was mad, but because she was still in pain. The next morning I drove to the hospital early and demanded an explanation from her doctor who said, "We think the Valium is the problem. We want to pull her off and see if her headaches get better."

He thought the Valium was *giving* her headaches. He never mentioned addiction. Well, I thought, that made sense. The Valium certainly had not made her headaches go away. But it was very difficult to sit in her room and watch her cry from the pain. It took four days but her headache went away.

She was released three days later. I checked her out of the hospital, loaded everything up and headed home. But in just minutes I realized she was acting extremely odd. Her back began to spasm. She started crying. She couldn't talk right. So I made a U-turn on the freeway and drove her back to the hospital.

I told the emergency room doctor I had just picked up my wife from their hospital and now I was bringing her back.

"Why?" they asked. "She looks fine."

"She's not fine," I fired back. We argued in front of my

wife who began having convulsions. They claimed it was nothing. I wound up telling the doctors I was going to leave her there. I was not taking her home. After six hours in the emergency room, they finally readmitted her and gave her a room. For observation. One thing I should point out here is that doctors are incredibly naive about drug withdrawal. No one—not a nurse, not a doctor, not an orderly—recognized what was happening.

That night in the hospital was really one of the most horrific nights of my life. I held Melissa for ten hours while she prayed, convulsed, hallucinated and nurses would cheerily come in, take her temperature and leave. It was by God's grace she didn't die then.

The next morning she began hearing voices. She heard her kids on the backyard swings. She heard her dead grandmother. She was transported to Billings, Montana to her grandmother's attic. She got up out of bed, looked out of the hospital window, and yelled at her invisible kids to be quiet.

At first I tried humoring her. She'd recognize me, then mentally leave. But soon I became more and more alarmed. I went to the nurses' station and suggested someone come in and listen to my wife. She was in full gear by the time a nurse arrived, having an argument with an invisible six-year-old. The nurses called a doctor. Then they told me to leave. But first, they gave her a Valium.

Over the next week, different doctors looked at her. A psychiatrist from a nearby mental hospital took over her case and started her on a declining dosage of Valium. In six more days, the day of her last Valium, I brought her home.

She had been gone now for two weeks. During that time I was busy getting the kids off to Mother's Day Out, or over to stay with neighbors. I was visiting Melissa in the hospital every morning and night; I was starting a company; I was leaving work early to be with my children; I was coaching soccer. The church was bringing us food every night. And I was petrified Melissa might not ever be the same. I thought I was coping.

Of course, Melissa's homecoming was short-lived. It was no longer her headaches; it was the shakes. The chills. Her hands began constricting. There were crying jags. And within a couple of days, she began convulsing again. The last day, her mother came over, very alarmed. We called the doctor who prescribed yet another tranquilizer, Haldol, for her convulsions. I jumped in my car, raced up to the drugstore, got the prescription filled, raced back home, stopped in the kitchen for a glass of water, and raced up the stairs with water and pills. I gave Melissa the water and was reading the prescription to her about "take one pill" when she grabbed the bottle and took three.

"What are you doing?" I yelled at her. It was beginning to dawn on me she was physically incapable of taking just one pill of anything. "The doctor said one pill every four hours," I said.

She never answered. She just got worse. Very nauseated. Bad muscle cramping. Hard arching in her back. Another call to the doctor.

"She's experiencing side effects," said the doctor, "bad side effects. You need to leave now and go get some Cogentin to counteract them. I'll call in a prescription."

Back downstairs. Back to the car. Back to the drugstore. Race back home. My heart's pounding; my wife is now more sick than ever and I'm scared out of my mind. Race the pills upstairs. Melissa grabs the bottle and takes three pills, to my horror.

"Melissa," I yelled at her. "Can't you ever just take one pill?"

She didn't hear me. She didn't hear anybody.

"Harry," her mother said, "I think we have a serious

problem. And if we don't take care of it, your wife is going to die."

I listened dumbfounded as her mother explained Melissa's obvious addiction to prescription drugs of all kinds—Valium, Demerol, Restoril, Seconal. All of it. How she was in drug withdrawal, and without help she was going to die.

At first my denial was simply too strong to accept it. My wife couldn't be an addict. That was for other people. There were no syringes in our house. "Look at her!" cried her mother in tears. "For God's sake, just look at her."

I saw a convulsing, crying, almost delirious woman lying in bed, unable to get up. Bathed in sweat. Gasping for breath. I saw my wife. I saw an addict.

That night we called treatment centers around the Southwest, but were unable to get her admitted immediately. In desperation, I remembered a new treatment center that no one knew anything about—but one month earlier, I had shot a commercial for them.

Baylor Parkside said yes, they could take her now. Just put her in the car and come. So I loaded up a shaking, quivering Melissa around 11:30 that night, and off we went to a town some thirty miles outside Dallas. Melissa spent the ride out there crying, saying how she couldn't be a drug addict, how she couldn't be like her mom and could we just turn around. It was about a forty-five minute drive and by the end of it, I was feeling a little stupid for racing my wife to a treatment center in the middle of the night. I began having doubts.

"We'll get through this," I told her. And took her hand.

Upon arrival, we were greeted by a male nurse who was very kind. He sat Melissa down and immediately took her blood pressure. Then he pulled out an admittance form and asked me to fill it out.

I looked up at him and said, "How do you know she's a

drug addict? Can you prove it? This is just a best guess, isn't it?"

He looked at me, he looked at Melissa who was arching her back, rubbing her legs, her arms, acting dazed and confused.

"I know something's wrong," I admitted, looking at her, "but how do you know it's drug addiction?"

I will never forget the next few moments. "Harry," he said taking a bottle of Valium out of his drawer, "the difference between drug addicts and the rest of us is that they don't take a pill or a snort or a shot because they want to—but because they have to. Here, Melissa." He pushed two Valiums towards her. "This will make you feel better."

As she gulped the pills, I persisted with my arguments. "You can't see this thing, you can't feel this thing, so how do you know what you're actually treating? There's no way you can prove any of this." He and I were still deep in discussion when I felt a tugging on my arm. It was Melissa.

"Harry," she said as she smoothed her hair and smiled for the first time in God knows when, "I feel fine now. Really. We can go home."

I looked at her in astonishment, at this woman who had been barely coherent minutes earlier, who had been near death back in Dallas. Chills went through my body. "No honey," I said as I pushed myself up from the table. "I think you're in the right place."

Melissa was in treatment for four weeks.

STEP ONE. We admitted we were powerless over alcohol and drugs—that our lives had become unmanageable.

*N*o one walks into Al-Anon because it's a boring Saturday night. It's always precipitated by a crisis. My crisis was simple. It wasn't that my wife was in a treatment center for drug addiction. It was that she was coming home.

Except for a wild four days at home, Melissa had been gone essentially six weeks. I came to believe that in the hospital she might die. I came to believe that in the treatment center she might not recover. Now she was coming home and I realized I was scared to death. I had been allowed to see her once a week at the treatment center. We would hold hands, walk around, play with the boys. But I could see she was changing.

I didn't know the change was drug withdrawal, but it was obvious she was becoming quite fragile, almost breakable. What was I supposed to do? How was I supposed to take care of her when she got home? Even worse, she had been gone *six weeks*. How were we supposed to make it all work? I had no idea. I wasn't even sure how to talk to her. It was suggested by several people I go to Al-Anon.

I had been to one Al-Anon meeting in the treatment center that left me convinced Al-Anon was nothing I wanted to get involved with. The treatment center had a rule that if you went to an Al-Anon meeting there on Sunday nights, you could talk to your wife afterward. So to earn the extra hour with my wife, I went to the "family hall" in the treatment center where the Al-Anon meeting was to be held. Instead of a huge crowd, there were only two women I had never seen before sitting prim and proper in their chairs.

"The things I do for Melissa," I thought to myself.

"Let's bring the meeting to order," one of them said.

"This is a meeting?" I thought.

The other one then read a very formalized, standard opening while I was thinking, "There are only three of us; let's just get this show on the road." Then, incredibly one woman asked if there were any announcements.

I put my head in my hands thinking, "Please Lord, let me get out of here soon." Thankfully there were none. Finally, the issue of a topic was put forth, and one of the two said, "Well, let's talk about why we are here."

And I said, "Well this is simple. I'm here because the treatment center said I could stay one hour longer with my wife if I came to this meeting."

The two women looked at me like I had lost my mind.

"Why are you here?" I politely inquired of the nearest woman.

"I'm here even though I divorced my alcoholic eight years ago," she said proudly.

I was in profound disbelief.

"What?" I asked. "You mean you don't live with him any more and you still come to these meetings?"

"Yes," she answered matter-of-factly, "Al-Anon helps me with everything in my life. I come to a meeting every week."

"Interesting," I said. Insane, I thought.

"Well, I'm here even though my alcoholic died five years ago," the other one said.

I looked at her like she said she had just seen a Martian.

I thought, well, I'm sitting with two of the loneliest, craziest women I have ever met. I was there in the Al-Anon meeting for a reason—to see my wife in fifteen minutes. For the life of me, I couldn't figure out why anybody who didn't have to would come to these dumb meetings.

So when people told me to go to Al-Anon, I had serious doubts, like any man would. But I also had a drug addict coming home that day.

I picked up the phone in my office and called the Al-Anon Central Office. They gave me the name and number of a man named Bill who had been in the program for a number of years. I called him at his office. He said he recommended I meet him at an Al-Anon meeting that very night.

I frankly don't remember a lot about Melissa's first night home. She looked incredibly frail. I told her I loved her, we all loved her, that we didn't hate her because of her drug addiction. But it was obvious she was ill at ease. She told me how much guilt she had, what a worthless person she thought she was, what a terrible mother she thought she was, what a terrible wife. Once again, I was confronted by the fact that no matter how much I loved my wife, how much pain I wanted to take away from her, there was nothing I could do. Except feel sick.

During the next few weeks, I could feel us drifting apart. She was going to recovery meetings every day, yet we seemed to be fighting more. She seemed to be consumed by a guilt I simply couldn't assuage. I couldn't say the right thing, or do the right thing. She would talk about how easy it would be to kill herself, how she fought the compulsion daily, how I didn't understand her pain. I would walk around on eggshells. She would break down in tears and tell me it wasn't me, but her. There would be days I couldn't touch her, couldn't hold her; then I'd say something and the raging would start.

Very early on, Bill told me I couldn't work her program,

only mine. That I was as sick—if not sicker—than she was. He said that in order to get her back I had to let her go; that to save my marriage I had to take my hands off of her. That to stay with her I had to detach from her, that I had to forget everything I had learned in my life up to now.

I went to several different meetings in several different clubs. But the one I most remember was where I first opened up and briefly told my story. I was frantic. I was worried about my wife. I was worried about my kids. I was worried about our marriage. I was worried about my company. I was worried about finances. I was so worried that I was having chest pains. I was literally sick with worry. I had that overwhelming feeling of anxiety, of worry, of something terrible that was about to happen which I couldn't stop.

And a woman stood up and looked at me and said, "Harry, you never have to feel this way again. Just come back."

I was stunned. She didn't know me from Adam but she knew how I felt.

And I had felt this way most of my life—that something was out of control that I should be able to control. I should be able to control how much money I make. I should be able to control my children. I should be able to control my marriage. I should be able to control my mother-in-law, my clients. I should be able to control our spending. I should be able to control my father, my weight, prospective clients I couldn't sell. I should be able to control the feelings of the guy who fired me. I should be able to control people's opinions of me. I should be able to control everything, but because everything was so out of control I was slowly going nuts. And this mysterious woman knew exactly how I felt.

This had nothing to do with Melissa being a drug addict. Feeling this way was normal for me. I would wake up in the morning feeling dread, fear and anxiety, and that was a normal morning. If I woke up feeling good, I would often lie in bed and search the cosmic airwaves with my antennae until I could remember what it was I was worried about the night before. "Oh that's it," I would tell myself. "Now I'm panic stricken."

And only then would I get out of bed. This feeling of anxiety, doom and gloom was normal. It was every day. It was part of me. And if I didn't feel it, I would miss it. But now here was this woman telling me I never had to feel this way again. And I had just told her my wife was a drug addict, our finances were shot, my two kids might never be normal, my marriage seemed to be dissolving, I had just been fired, and she could say, "You never have to feel this way again."

That was enough for me. I thought I might come back.

Shortly after that I asked Bill to be my sponsor. In the program, this is sort of like a spiritual guide. We would meet at least once a week and discuss the steps. He pointed out that the steps in AA are identical to the steps in Al-Anon.

"You're very much like your wife," he told me one night.

I was mystified.

"You're an addict too. Only your drug is different."

My wife was addicted to a class of tranquilizers called benzodiazepines, though in reality both of us believe she could have become addicted to rutabaga, given the opportunity. I, on the other hand, had become addicted to a class of behavior encompassing control, fear and criticism—drugs just as powerful as benzodiazepines and just as dangerous.

"It will be harder for you to stop," he said.

I thought he wasn't giving me enough credit for being able to change. It turned out he was being generous.

We talked about the First Step: admitted we were power-less over alcohol, that our lives had become unmanageable.

Bill started off, "You know what it means when addicts say they're powerless over drugs—that's fairly clear—they can't control it; they can't control the cravings for it; they can't control their actions when they use it; they can't control how much they use of it."

Then he looked at me. "Can you admit you're powerless too?"

"Over what?" I asked him.

"Over everything," he replied.

"No," I said coolly. "I cannot admit that."

And I couldn't. He wanted me to admit that not only was I powerless over drugs and Melissa's craving for the drugs, he wanted me to admit I was powerless over *everything*.

This contradicted everything I learned in life about being a man, being in control. Men are supposed to be in control of everything. Al-Anon teaches us we're in control of nothing.

I never realized control might be an issue until I started working the steps. I could accept my life was unmanageable, but the First Step also says we're powerless over *everything*. For months, I had many long talks about this with my sponsor.

Bill had me first list all the things I was in control of and believe me there was a list. I had control over taking care of the kids, waking them, feeding them breakfast, taking them to day care, entertaining them when I got home, bathing them, putting them to bed. I had control over household finances, over the appearance of the yard; I controlled the boys' soccer teams, my company, the older one's homework. I had to read to the boys at night, be vigilant about their TV, help my wife with everything from dinner to dealing with her mother, to just holding her in the middle of the night while she mysteriously cried. When I thought about it, I had a pretty firm hand on everything.

Then he had me list the things that were rapidly going out of control. Well, clearly, my life was out of control. My marriage was out of control, in spite of my best efforts. My finances were out of control. I seemingly was losing control of my boys' lives. This soccer thing was out of control. In fact I was having severe disagreements with the board of directors of the league. I felt like our spending was out of control. *The fact was, everything I felt I needed to have control over was out of control.* Or, said another way, everything I felt powerless over was what I felt like I had to have power over.

Indeed the only thing that seemed to be going well was Melissa's recovery. And I had nothing to do with that.

We talked about this list.

I couldn't accept I was powerless over everything. My wife and kids would die if that were true. To keep that from happening, I needed all the power in the world.

It took many years to realize where my control instincts came from: my father. I remember one strange day when he was driving me to high school, and some kid peeled out of the parking lot laying maybe fifty feet of rubber.

"Why did he do that?" my father started yelling at me. "Why do kids do that? Don't they know how much tires cost?"

I had not a clue. I had just turned fifteen. But he yelled at me all the way to school, then brought the matter up again that night. And this is just one incident from a very strange upbringing. But I learned very early that if I could control things, perhaps I wouldn't be yelled at.

Control is a symptom of fear, pure and simple. If I was in fear of something happening or not happening, I learned to try and control it. I had been doing that all my life. I tried to control my wife's circumstances, so she could be happy all the time. That meant I tried to control every minute of her every day, because if she made the wrong decision, that could result in a headache or worse. I tried to make sure that she only made the right decisions (or decisions that I thought were right) because I loved her, not because I hated her. Because I worried about her, felt for her. When she was in pain, I was in pain. For me to avoid pain, I had to help her avoid pain. Of course, that only causes more problems.

I felt my children's lives had to be controlled or something bad could happen to them. For instance, two years before my wife went into a treatment center, my four-year-old son wanted to join a soccer team. I called the soccer association and was told he could be placed on a team, but that the team needed a coach. Did I know one?

Now, being from Texas, I know what coaches are like. They yell, scream and intimidate the kids. So, to keep my oldest son from having that kind of coach, I became a soccer coach—and in the process, became the exact kind of coach I never wanted my son to have. I made him center forward. I built the team around him. I demanded that he score. I pushed him to try harder. And he did his level, four-and five-year-old best. I joined the soccer board; became a director and commissioner. I didn't know what offsides was, but I had lots of control. At least I thought so.

Then came one game where he simply couldn't do what I asked. He had other five-year-old issues, and they didn't include pounding the ball into a net fifty yards away. In fact, he simply didn't care about the game or that he needed to score and I was enraged. On the way home, I tried to control my anger, but I kept verbally jabbing at him. About how he needed to try harder. About how he disappointed me.

Later that night, while putting him to bed, I let him have it again. And again. And again. I guess if he had started crying, I would have stopped, but he never did. So I kept on. And my wife, ripped as she was on Valium, stormed up the stairs and asked, "What does it matter he didn't score? He's five years old."

And I remember yelling back that it matters because I *try*. "I go to two practices a week, I go to one game a week, I go to soccer meetings, board meetings, serve as a commissioner—he owes it to me!"

She glared at me. "You're crazy. He doesn't owe you a thing; he's five years old."

She was right. She was at the beginning of her addiction; she was probably stoned out of her mind and she was right.

Coaching soccer was one example of my control issues gone wild. So one step to recovery for me was giving it up. And it was astonishing to learn that my kids could actually play better for another coach who wasn't nearly as bizarre as I was. (And it was strange to sit on the sidelines and watch opposing coaches diagram plays on clipboards for thoroughly befuddled four-year-olds. Sickos, I thought. Just like me.)

Control was my addiction. When I came home from work I would always go straight to the kitchen and open the lids of the pots on the stove to see what my wife was cooking. I just thought she needed help. I told her where to clean and when. I drove her everywhere on weekends because I was fearful for her safety. I told her what to buy and when. I kept the checkbook and doled out cash to her every week.

I had her call me at the office to tell me her movements. I would monitor her TV shows so she wouldn't watch anything too scary or sad (but she could cry at Toyota commercials). I wouldn't show her the newspaper if the headlines looked too frightening. (But the grislier the news, the better she liked it, even to this day. And it still is a mystery to me.) When it came to movies, I was the censor board.

Nothing too frightening or sad (a movie like *Love Story* was totally unacceptable, if for no other reason than Melissa would believe she too had leukemia). Why? Because I was afraid she would cry and if she did, I would somehow be responsible.

But it doesn't matter how honorable your intentions. Control is control.

I tried to control my wife's relationship with her kids, especially the older one with whom she would have the most amazing arguments, even when he was four. I would always patch up the fights, make them hug each other, make them apologize.

And of course, I tried to control what she thought of me. Some of our biggest fights were prompted by her telling me I was a worthless husband. In fact she would often rage at me so viciously it would leave me shaken. So then I would proceed to explain to her that only a Saint Francis of Assisi like me could live with her and we'd just go to town from there. It seemed like the more I tried to control what she thought of me, the less she thought of me.

And it was the same way with my boss. I had killed myself to make him think I was a hardworking genius, fanatically loyal to his company. And I wound up getting fired. The harder I tried to control what people thought of me, the less they thought of me.

This is just a small sample, yet I could look my sponsor in the eye and say "I just don't know if I really have any control issues."

Al-Anon teaches us to let go of control. It teaches us that we are powerless over essentially everyone and everything. We are powerless over the guy who cuts us off in traffic, so why get into a yelling match with him? We are powerless over our spouses, so why try to change them? We are powerless over the airplane we're flying in, so why freak out for two hours? Al-Anon teaches us we're powerless over what our elderly parents say and think, so why let it upset us? Al-Anon teaches us we're powerless over what other people think of us, so why worry about it?

We learn that we are ultimately powerless over other people—including, especially our wives and children, which means they can survive if we give them the space and the room. Learning that we're powerless teaches us the astonishing miracle of detachment.

Detachment is nothing more than realizing you are not God, that you don't know what's best for everybody and that the only person you have any control over at any time is yourself. Detachment means you're not responsible. You're blameless. You're not involved. Detachment means you don't have to control what other people think, do, say, drink, shoot up, run around with. Detachment means things you thought were problems aren't anymore, because they are simply not your problems.

Detachment means your wife's recovery is her problem. The only thing you can do to help her is not stand in the way of her going to meetings. Incredibly, many husbands simply cannot accept the fact that other people—sometimes truly outlandish people—are better equipped to get their wives sober than the husbands are. So they prevent their wives from going to meetings, either through manipulation or outright hostility. Inevitably, their wives use or drink again.

Detachment means you don't have to take personally anything the drug addict says to you. Al-Anon teaches us that the drug addict or alcoholic will say the cruelest things because they hate themselves. And for the moment, they've turned that hate on you. I also learned it was okay if Melissa said she hated me, because that's how she felt at that point in time. And not being God, I did not have the capability of changing her mind. The best thing I could do was encourage her to call her sponsor, not say anything I'd regret, then pick up the paper, mow the yard, go jogging, whatever. This is one of the hardest lessons to accept. People are entitled to their own opinions—you are not in control of what other people think. Even your wife. If she hates you right now, let her. Arguing with her will not change her mind. An AA meeting probably will.

Detachment means you don't have to participate in a crazed alcoholic or drug-hazed argument. You can leave. I never knew I could leave. I thought I had to convince my wife of the error of her ways, even if it took screaming all night. My sponsor told me that the next time my wife lost control, started raging and screaming and saying cruel and hostile things, not to listen. Leave! What an incredible idea! Don't listen to hate and raging and bitter sarcasm. Leave!

What made this such a great idea is that in the past, I would listen to her rages, file everything away and then hold on to the anger and resentment for several years. I could remember the slightest jab for months, not to mention a truly well-aimed blow. Several months into recovery, I learned the technique of leaving any argument and soon had the opportunity to try it. I have no idea what the fight started over, except she had been three months without drugs and was really, truly unhappy. So the fight started. And I once again was defending myself against charges of being a worthless and terrible husband when I suddenly remembered I wasn't going to win this or any argument. In fact, it was only going to get worse. So I said, "I'm not going to get into a fight about this." And I got up and left the room.

Well, what my sponsor didn't tell me is that when you leave an argument with a drug addict who's three months into a recovery, you're just going to make them madder. They don't want you to leave. They want you to fight with them. So they follow you from room to room. Melissa followed me all over the house. Yelling. She would have followed me up into the attic if I had gone there. So my first attempts at leaving an argument, while not totally successful, did have the desired impact. Our fights began ending faster, with much less blood on the walls.

But again, drug addicts and alcoholics are not keen on your detachment. They hate it. Your presence, your worrying, your interfering actually serves a legitimate purpose— it makes you the bad guy. They may be ripped on coke or bombed on whiskey, but the moment you say you've "had enough," or "let's put the bottle away," congratulations, *your* behavior is now the problem, not theirs.

Your interference and meddling and criticism are now the issues, not their using. So they would rather you not detach because now they have no one to blame, your side of the street is clean. Melissa actually went to our priest over this idea of detachment and reported back to me he was against it, that a husband should never detach from his wife.

Through the miracle of detachment, I was able to ignore this. I at first felt hurt, but then I realized a drug addict is one of the world's greatest cons (my wife had eighty active prescriptions from at least three doctors by the time she was put in treatment). I realized our priest was woefully ignorant of drug addiction. In fact it wasn't even worth getting mad over. So I didn't. I detached. And avoided another fight.

To admit we are powerless is to detach. To walk away from an argument is to detach. To let your wife jab at you without defending yourself is to detach. We aren't born with this ability. But we can't live without it. Just how important is detachment to your recovery and your marriage? Well, three months home from the treatment center Melissa told me she didn't know if she loved me anymore. That she'd met a guy at treatment. A drug addict. She thought she might be in love with him.

STEP TWO. Came to believe that a Power greater than ourselves could restore us to sanity.

*T*he essence of Step One is learning we're powerless and that efforts to control the uncontrollable have made our lives chaotic. Step Two just comes right out and tells us we're not well. In fact, that we're insane. No matter if your wife is the drug user, you're insane. And of course, a power greater than ourselves is the solution.

At first glance, the temptation is to say, "Why not just say God could restore us to sanity?" Well, because at this stage he can't. We won't let him. The reason is, by the time we find our way to recovery, we have a lot of gods. And all they do is get us into trouble. We can't be restored to sanity until we have the right God to help us.

I was told to make a list of powers greater than myself. It was a disturbingly long list. My wife was my higher power. I tried to make her happy, I tried to let her never get upset, I worried about her constantly, but most of all, I cared desperately about what she thought of me. I cared more about what she thought of me than what God thought of me, than even what *I* thought of me. Because if she thought I was terrible, I was terrible. If she thought I was terrific, then I was terrific.

Every boss I had became my higher power. I cared very much about what they thought of me. I would act one of two ways around them: agree with everything they said so they would think I was easy to get along with, or disagree with them constantly to show I was an independent thinker.

Success was also my higher power. I would read in industry magazines about how people my age or younger were getting promoted, doing well in their jobs. I would be filled with jealousy and loathing. For them. For me. For my situation.

Clients became my higher power, because I gave them power of life and death over me. If a client was happy, he'd use me again. We could eat, pay the mortgage and so on. If a client was unhappy, I'd have to sell everything I owned and move into a station wagon. You can see how easy it was for me to make clients or bosses my higher power; they possessed the power of God over me.

I wrote down that my father had been my higher power while I was growing up, because I was deathly afraid of his temper—I was convinced he had powers of life and death over me.

My children were my higher powers. Not just because I cared so much about them, but because I wanted to be more than a good father—I wanted to be the *perfect* father. I cared very much what they thought of me and what they would come to think of me. I hoped that by the time they were four, they would come to realize how hard I was trying to be a perfect father. It would kill me if they thought of me the way I thought of my own father.

My jobs had been higher powers, money was a higher power, success was a higher power, financial security was a higher power, there were friends whose opinions of me I held sacred and they were my higher powers. In fact, I was fairly dripping with higher powers. Then there was God.

I had just never really considered that I had put so many other people and things on his plane. Regrettably, I rarely thought about God except to blame him. But the opinions of my wife, my children, my bosses, my friends—these could make or break me. Success, fortune, money—I felt they could make me happy. If only God would let me have them.

It was suggested that I narrow down this list of higher powers to one. To God. To a power truly greater than myself.

But saying it is one thing. Doing it is another.

Why do Al-Anons especially collect a number of gods? I think one reason is that we learn to give some people power over us. It could happen in childhood when a drunk father or mother does indeed hold in their hands the power to kill us. So we got used to the idea of making them our higher power. And then for some unfathomable reason, we go out into the world in search of people just like them to give them power over us.

It is probably in childhood when we come up with the idea that if I can just control this situation, I might get out of this day alive. We may well decide then that the more difficult a person or a situation is, the more we are drawn to them. We subconsciously think that one of these days, one of these higher powers is going to say you did a good job, or I forgive you, or tell me they love me, or if I succeed I can be happy. Then I can get all the things successful people get; then people will respect me.

Whatever the reason, I collected gods like some kids collect baseball cards.

Obviously you can't be married to a god. Especially if she's a recovering drug addict, who thinks she might be in love with another one. That can make you do truly crazy, *insane* things. So I had to make a conscious effort to turn my higher powers back into ordinary people. To turn fame, fortune and financial security into circumstances, not gods. To turn my father back into a man. My friends back into people. My ex-bosses back into humans. My wife back into a woman. I found I didn't have nearly so many expectations of people once they were no longer gods.

Expectations were one of my biggest problems. I expected my wife to be a cross between the playmate of the month and president of the Episcopal women's group. I expected her to like football. I expected her to like my friends. I expected her not to be jealous of the women I worked with. I expected her not to spend a lot of money. I expected her to always be sweet and kind, especially to me. But most of all, I expected her to be happy. Because if she was happy, I was happy. And keeping her happy was driving me crazy.

It simply couldn't be done. I would buy her a Cadillac, thinking—this is it, now she'll be happy. And the next day she wouldn't be happy with her refrigerator. I was just dumbfounded about how she could always be so unhappy. I'd take her on vacation, we'd have a great time, and she'd be unhappy when we got home. I'd buy her a fur coat, and she'd be unhappy with the dining room table. I kept expecting that I could eventually spend enough money to make her so happy she would never want anything again.

If I hadn't been so nuts, I might have realized it's okay for her to want things, and not to get them. It's not just okay, it's normal. And just because I can't give her everything she wants doesn't mean I don't love her to pieces, and that she won't love me.

Somewhere in my mind, I figured she wouldn't love me unless I got her everything she ever wanted. She never told me that. I just deduced that all by myself.

I expected my kids to be great kids. Kids who were happy. I expected my sons to be their teams' leading scorers. I expected them to do well in school. I expected them to never fight, learn Spanish from the maid, but above all, to be happy.

I expected my bosses to shower me with praise and

money. My peers to recognize my talent. And I fully expected to be wildly successful, rich and powerful—though I would be at a loss to describe what powerful meant.

But clearly, my expectations led to my anointing many different higher powers. And that's a rule of life: if you build up all these great expectations—for yourself and for other people—your hopes will be dashed by reality. Then you become frustrated, and control takes over. Expectations turn into demands, which, when left unmet, leads to anger. So we try to control the situation even harder; we start manipulating, scheming, plotting. But worst of all, we think about it all the time. We have mind conversations, imagined arguments, fantasy fights. Some of these we actually win, some we lose.

All this strikes at the heart of Step Two. We are insane. We're letting a drug addict control our lives. We're letting a four-year-old control our lives. We're letting a boss who fired us ten years earlier control our lives. We're getting upset with some guy 2000 miles away for getting a promotion—a guy who doesn't even know we're alive. We are nuts. I was nuts. And insane thinking only leads to more insanity. I expected Melissa to tell me truthfully she no longer cared about the man she met at the treatment center. I expected this epiphany every day for six months. Which only led to her lying about the end of their relationship.

So when my sponsor asked me to write down what was insane about my life, I had a full plate: not only was my wife seemingly in love with another drug addict, the insurance company wasn't honoring my wife's $20,000 hospitalization claim. I was coaching not one, but two youth soccer teams two days a week, with two games on Saturday. I was teaching Sunday school, going to soccer board meetings. I was going to Al-Anon meetings twice a week, trying to get a company off the ground, frantically searching for clients, petrified I was going to lose our house.

I'd wake up every morning and my wife would announce, "Today I think I'll kill myself." I was going to PTA meetings, listening to my wife's rages, trying to be a perfect father, trying to be a perfect husband. I was angry at the world because I couldn't be successful faster. I was going crazy at work between deciding whether to work late because I was desperately behind, or get home as fast as I could because Melissa and the boys couldn't be alone together for too long. I was waking up early and feeding the boys breakfast, taking them to Mother's Day Out, phoning home five, six times a day to make sure everything was all right. After I finished this list it became quite apparent I had gone over the edge. And the only one who could deliver me from this chaos was a power demonstrably greater than I. Someone who created the universe.

God.

STEP THREE. Made a decision to turn our will and our lives over to the care of God *as we understood Him.*

*G*od. The steps always bring us back to God. Many of us have truly twisted versions of God. The God I grew up with was not a God I wanted to turn my will and my life over to—this God would kill me. And this became more and more apparent to me over the first six months in the program. My sponsor would ask me if I was ready to turn my will and my life over to God, and I would say absolutely not.

He would ask me why not and I would say the same thing: I don't trust him. I would pray to God. I would talk to God. But I couldn't bring myself to trust God.

I always had an odd relationship with God. Early in our marriage I would walk outside and scream at him, "What do you want? What?"

I would scream at him over our financial health, over my marriage, over work. I would scream at him when the car broke down and we couldn't fix it. I would scream at him when I felt that he might stab me in the back just when everything was going well. I would hold him accountable, attributable, responsible for my life. I would pray he would help me with my mortgage, with our car payments, with life. I would demand he get busy. I would get mad, I would plead, I would beg, I would cry but nothing would change.

So about six months into the program, it was becoming apparent that this "thing" between my wife and her boyfriend was getting to be more, not less of a problem, that my job situation was becoming more critical because I needed more money, that my obsessiveness about being the perfect soccer commissioner had resulted in my being brought up in front of the disciplinary committee, that my whole life appeared to be unraveling and my sponsor recommended that I think about turning my will and my life over to God because clearly I had screwed the whole thing up.

And once again, I replied that as bad as I had obviously screwed everything up, God would only make it worse. So my sponsor suggested that maybe I was now ready to work on this God thing. He asked me that night to write down what kind of god my God was. What was his personality? What was he like?

I retired to a quiet place in our house and wrote down that God was a liar who couldn't be trusted. He went out of his way to stab me in the back. He ignored my prayers and pleadings. He would set me up only to let me fall. That he didn't care about me, that he didn't love me, that he was the invisible task-master whose job was to punish me for past and current sins. I felt if I turned my will and my life over to God, he would move me to Calcutta to work with Mother Teresa. I wrote that I prayed to God because he would punish me if I didn't.

I wrote that God would go through periods where he would shower me with misfortune. He didn't want me to be happy; he really didn't want to see me succeed; he loved other people more than me; he thought nothing of ruining my marriage, shattering my kids' lives; he enjoyed scaring me to death. And that basically, no matter how hard I tried, I couldn't please him.

I read this litany over the phone to my sponsor that night. He listened impassively until I finished.

"Gee, Harry," he said, "your God sounds like an alcoholic. Your God sounds like your father."

Well, this absolutely stunned me. I read the list again. Yes, God did appear to have the characteristics of an alcoholic. I remember closing my eyes thinking, "What have I done?"

"That's the God you grew up with," my sponsor told me. "I wouldn't turn my will and my life over to that God either. Now go write down the God you would like to have."

Okay, this was a strange request, but taking the same legal pad I had used to describe my current God, I flipped the page over and began writing the kind of God I would like to have. A kind God. A patient God. A loving God. A forgiving God. A God who would be near me all the time, who would comfort me and console me. A God who wouldn't judge, who wouldn't punish, who wouldn't rage. A God I could trust. A God who cared about me. Who cared about my family. Who cared about my happiness.

I wanted a God who wouldn't hold me responsible for the acts of the world, a God I could talk to, that I didn't have to say the perfect prayer to—a God who wouldn't stab me in the back but help me go forward. I wanted a God who was sober, who knew I was in trouble before I told him—a God powerful enough to direct my life, but loving enough to be trusted. Not a vengeful God, but a tender God. A God I could relax around.

I called my sponsor and read him my new list.

"That's your God, Harry," he quietly told me. "That's the God of your understanding."

I prayed to my new God that night for the first time. I prayed without fear or dread or hopelessness. I stayed in his presence for maybe an hour, and even then I was reluctant to leave it. I felt a new peace and glow. I experienced incarnate love and forgiveness for the first time. I said thank you over and over. I felt freed; I felt a rebirth.

This was a God I could turn my will and my life over to: my will for my marriage, my children, my company, our house, our health, our future, the boys' happiness, the soccer hearings, Melissa's relationship with this guy, my finances, her addiction, my insanity. This was a God I could turn all of my life over to: my past life, my mistakes, my sins, my errors, my failures, my disappointments, my burdens, my future life, my present life, my fears, my concerns. This was a God I never had, even though he had always been there.

My God was no longer a raging alcoholic. My God was God.

Discovering a loving God makes an immediate impact on one's life. Not a Jesus freak, everything-is-groovy impact, but maybe-I-can-relax-a-moment impact. Until then, fear was my constant companion. Fear of the known, fear of the unknown. Fear of the future, fear of the past. Fear was my motivation in life—fear of failure, fear of losing our house, fear of losing my wife, fear of losing my family, fear of becoming a street person, fear of living in a Chevrolet, fear of making the wrong decision, fear of relaxing even for a second because the whole goddamn world could cave in on you while you were relaxing.

If for a strange moment I wasn't in fear, something would inevitably happen that would make me terrified. I could be peacefully jogging down a street in one of the most expensive residential areas in town—fall day, leaves turning, cool and crisp, a day when you're glad to be alive. I could be jogging down this street, reveling in a presentation that went right, or a piece of new business we had landed—I mean everything would be perfect.

Then I'd pass a picture-perfect little $400,000 cottage with a trike in front and my mind would follow this kind of logic in the space of, say, fifty feet: "Nice house. Like the shutters. Hey, there's a trike. A kid must live here. Hope he rides on the sidewalk. What would happen if he rode his trike in the street? Well, he could get killed on this street if a car came barreling down....I wonder where my boy is. Oh, God, I hope he isn't on his trike. In the middle of our street!" Then I would be transported instantly to the funeral.

So I would make a U-turn in the middle of my run, sprint back to the YMCA, grab the phone from the astonished attendant, frantically call my wife and all but yell, "Get Field off his trike!" and my wife would quietly tell me both boys were taking a nap.

So I'd stand there dripping wet in the middle of the Y, having barely survived another crisis. And I did this time after time after time. If, God forbid, she didn't answer the phone, I would just know she and the boys were at the emergency room. And I'd be in stark terror.

Fear haunted my life. For the longest time, I would lie awake at night listening to sounds in the house. I did this for years. I'd search the house with my heart pounding and always find the same thing: nothing.

I was deathly afraid of having a heart attack. Not so much because of fear of death, but because of the agony I knew I'd put my wife and kids through. Which, when I thought about it, gave me chest pains. Time after time after time I would rush to the hospital—in a cab if I was out of town, or driven by my wife or business associates in town—convinced I was dying of a heart attack. My chest would hurt. My arm would hurt. I would be hyperventilating. I would be terrified.

I would be fine.

I've had more middle-of-the-night electrocardiograms than are necessary in most rest homes. I've been to emergency rooms in Los Angeles, San Francisco and Dallas. I became a legend at my cardiologist's office—the one who prescribed panic medicine for me. I ran up to six miles a day, lifted weights, lost forty pounds all in an effort to ease my fear of having a heart attack. All to no avail. I practiced TM. I prayed. I would get mad at God. Nothing worked.

Except Step Three.

Fear kept me from balancing my checkbook for three years, because I was fearful of knowing how much money I didn't have. Such a clever financial decision resulted in my absorbing over $4000 in overdraft charges alone because we bounced over $22,000 in checks, and virtually wiped out our savings account.

This kind of all-encompassing, mind-boggling fear isn't a lack of faith. It's a lack of God. And it's a fear I lived with for a very long time. No doubt I was afraid something bad would happen to my wife if I didn't help her cook her dinner, if I didn't tell her whom to talk to, if I didn't encourage her to join tennis clubs, if I didn't try and make her into the kind of person I thought she needed to be to keep her out of pain. And of course, this only caused a great deal more pain.

So, once I had a God I could trust, I could begin to turn my fears over to him. "Leave them there," my sponsor would counsel. "Leave them with God; don't pick them back up." Well, it takes a serious faith to do that. But faith in God—and I'm not talking about a faith that there is a God—but faith that God loves you, cherishes you, wants to protect you; this kind of faith doesn't come easily for a lot of people. I've found it kind of like sticking your foot in an ice cold lake.

"Okay," I told God, "you can have these fears."

I lied. He knew I was lying. He knew I wasn't going to just change instantly. But I do truly believe he appreciates the effort. So I tried to give him my fears. I still do, even today. He still knows I'm lying. Just not as bad. Fear that I might not be in control, that the very worst will happen if I let go, this is something I battle every day, just as Melissa battles her drug addiction. Fear of something happening to my family, fear that my wife will be unhappy or that my kids might lack for something and be forever scarred—this fear is always with me, always in the background of my mind pushing me, driving me—and the only release is consciously turning everything over to God.

Sometimes I battle fear on an hourly basis. Like during a crisis at work, or an emergency. Just recently, my wife called me and said our youngest son was injured in a diving accident and to meet her at the emergency room. I worked downtown, twenty-four miles from our hospital. I learned several things on the trip home: one, that you can pray doing 120 mph on a tollroad; two, God still hears you; and three, I still have more work to do with fear. But I am getting better.

We've been through some very scary financial times, but I've always had a feeling God would create a miracle. And he always has. Sometimes the miracle is a check, sometimes it's a new account, sometimes the miracle is that we didn't need a miracle at all, that all we had to do was make some changes in our spending and everything was fine. But God has never let me down. Never. And if I can remind myself of that fact daily—or when necessary, hourly—then I can stay calm and serene. I have learned, as we all learn, that I can do the task in front of me and leave the results to him. That's one of the precepts of Al-Anon. And it's the truth.

When people talk about "doing the steps," what they mean is that a sponsor is having them write, having them think, having them feel pain they don't want to feel. This is what was happening with me doing Step Three. I had to be realistic about fears. I had to develop a new God. I had to develop a new relationship with God. I had to learn to trust him and give him my will and my life. And ultimately, I had to deal with my wife and this guy. Because my wife could no longer be my higher power. And I had to face the fact I couldn't live this way, that she might leave, that my greatest fear—losing my wife—might actually happen.

When you start "doing the steps," something weird happens. You become less able to carry a grudge; you have to deal with issues as they come up. Well, I had been refusing to deal with Melissa and this "boyfriend thing" since she came home from treatment. She would tell me about him, and I would say "it will pass." We would talk and she would swear it was nothing, that she wouldn't see him anymore. And of course, she would. I would know it. I could feel it. There'd be phone calls. There would be times she'd be gone. But the very strange thing was *I never got mad.* Maybe the fear of losing her was just too great.

I look back at those days and wonder just how crazy I was or was becoming. But Step Three puts an end to that craziness. Step Three is very definitive about turning your life over to God, not your wife. Step Three meant that one morning, out of the blue, I started getting mad. I talked to Melissa again about this guy. Yes, she had been seeing him again. I got up, walked outside, and for the first time since she had given me that news six months earlier, I started crying. Sobbing. All the frustration and fear and resentment and jealousy and rage I had been feeling came pouring out. I couldn't stop.

Melissa came running out and for the first time in our marriage I couldn't stand her touching me. I sat down in the alley and cried and cried and cried. And I told her I couldn't take it anymore. I told her she could leave. That I would take the boys and the house and the furniture and the cars and she could take her drug addict boyfriend and get out of our lives. If she thought a judge was going to give a drug addict control of the kids she was out of her mind. I said I was fed up, through, so leave. Please God, just get out of my life. I don't want to see you again. Leave. Now.

And of course, this is when I saved our marriage.

She started crying. She started saying how she never meant to hurt me. How she never wanted to hurt me or the boys. I screamed that she had spent six months ripping my heart out, so please leave. She said she wanted to kill herself. I told her I was tired of hearing that. I told her I was sick of the suicide threats, sick of her threatening to leave, sick of her boyfriend. I told her again to leave.

She said she wanted to stay. I said no. She pleaded to stay. I said no. She asked what she could do to stay. I said she could never see him again. Ever. Because if she did, I would kill him. And throw her out. That means never. That means one time and you're gone and I get everything. I told her I never wanted to go through this pain again, that I was tired of the lying, and that if she ever once crossed me on this, our marriage was over, and she could try living on a drug addict's income.

Stunned, she said, "Let me get this straight. I can never see him again?"

"Yes," I replied.

"And if I do, our marriage is over and you get *everything*."

"After I kill him," I corrected her. "Our marriage is over and I get the boys, the house, the cars, everything."

We looked at each other through tear-stained eyes. "I want to stay," she said.

"I can't live like this anymore," I said. "I won't. I can't."

"I want to stay," she repeated. "I want to stay."

That was it. Melissa was no longer my higher power. She was my wife. Maybe for the first time.

STEP FOUR. Made a searching and fearless moral inventory of ourselves.

*R*ecovery is reality-based. We cannot go along in this life expecting a sane marriage, all the while blaming our husband or wife—no matter how much alcohol or pills they consume—for our own unhappiness. The fact is, Melissa and I chose each other not just on a physical plane, but on a spiritual one as well. I chose Melissa. She chose me.

At one time in college my girlfriend was a Phi Beta Kappa, a class favorite, a campus beauty and I was bored silly. I dumped her—this was college, mind you—for a suicidal, alcoholic, sexually active girl who scared me to death with threats of suicide, telling me her dark dreams and clinging to me possessively. This was five years before I met Melissa. And I was already looking for her.

To make a searching and fearless inventory of ourselves is to open ourselves up to the fact that maybe we're not perfect. That maybe the problem is us. That just maybe, our wives are popping five to ten tranquilizers a day just to live with us. Or worse, that in some weird, mystical way, they're getting sicker because that's what we want them to do.

How could I marry a drug addict? Because it was the only kind of woman I was drawn to; because I found them exciting, challenging, stimulating; because the sex was great; because I wanted to. When I started taking an honest look at the women I had dated, I was astonished. The only kind of woman I was interested in drank a lot, had wild swings in mood, often broke my heart or completely dominated my time. Nice, normal, straight girls, I had no interest in. Ever.

Even today, I can walk into a restaurant and I can positively identify the female drug addicts just by studying the tables. It's kismet, it's mystical, but our hearts leap toward each other, dance around the room—and she may not have even looked up. I can walk into an AA meeting and fall in love four or five times in ten seconds. I can spot the drug addicts; I'm drawn to them like moths to a flame, and I am never, ever wrong.

That's why in Al-Anon we're told: even though the first year of recovery will be difficult, don't get divorced because you'll just sprint right out and find somebody worse. It happens without fail, all the time. So we're told to spend a year working on ourselves, getting better, then if a divorce is unavoidable, okay. At least we'll have the tools to appreciate sanity and sobriety. Then, even though we may be drawn to the flame, we won't have to fly in.

That was what the Fourth Step revealed to me. I had to take an honest look at my life, from as far back as I could remember. This was easier said than done. My brother and I often joked how we had no memory of our early childhood. None. We were like kids from some science fiction show dropped into 1965. We had pretty clear memories of high school, but nothing before that. And my clearest memory in high school was of my mother dying.

I cannot remember junior high or grade school friends, or events or parties or supposedly significant happenings. I can't remember my grandmother's house or my aunt's. I can't remember my bedrooms; I can't remember our old houses; I can't remember eating dinner with my family when I was young. I can't remember teachers; I can't remember dad's cars; I can't remember going out with my family. I can barely remember vacations (not so much where, as the fact that we went), and I sure can't remember anything before the age of thirteen. My brother's the same way.

The great thing about Al-Anon meetings is that basically we're all alike. If you come and pay attention, you'll hear your story coming from some other guy. I'll never forget the Al-Anon meeting where one guy said he had no memory of his childhood either, because he always lived in the future. Wham! I instantly knew what he was talking about. I had spent most of my life living in the future. Either being scared silly over something bad that might happen, or fantasizing over some dream that I wished would happen. I spent so much time in fear or fantasy that I was never there for the present moment. No wonder I had no childhood memories. I wasn't mentally around.

My father raged and threatened a lot, which kept me in fear. Sometimes I was afraid he would get mad; sometimes I would be afraid that he would kill me; sometimes I would be afraid that he was about to go stark raving mad. I remember one vacation we took as a family where he got lost trying to get on an interstate and wound up on a dead end service road with the freeway above him. He started laughing like a banshee, floored the car and went straight up a fifty foot incline to get on the freeway. This was in a Chevrolet, in 1955 when only the army had jeeps. I knew I was going to die that night.

The point is, being in constant fear of his fear kept me out of the present moment. I could never just enjoy the moment because I kept dwelling on just how horrible the future might be.

But then I learned a way to stay out of fear—fantasize. This works every time. Fantasize about what a great guy you are, about how people like you, about what a star you might be, or worse—buy into your alcoholic father's fantasies. And he had plenty. He would tell us that we were going to inherit half of downtown Dallas; that he was going to buy us a boat for making good grades; that he was going to do a mega deal with the Saudis; that we would inherit a fortune through his efforts.

So I was living either in fear of the future, or fantasizing about it. That's why I don't really recall that much about my childhood.

But one night I was having dinner with my sponsor, thinking that the evening was going well, when he looked up at me and said, "I think you're the angriest person I've ever met." This blew my mind, because I had not uttered one negative word about anyone that night.

He said my fear was anger turned inward and that until I dealt with my anger, I could never get rid of my demons. He said it was time to do the Fourth Step, which in the program is when you go back through history and write down every time you got mad or jealous or angry with another person and why.

I asked, "Every time?"

He said, "Every time."

"How far back do I go?"

"To birth," he quipped. "Or in your case, maybe further."

"But I don't remember a thing."

"Try it," he assured me. "It always works."

"Okay," I acquiesced. This couldn't take too long, I reasoned. Since I didn't remember anything, I could do this during the commercials on "Cheers."

"One last thing," he cautioned. "The shortest Fifth Step I ever heard was twenty-five minutes."

"Yeah?"

"He was a paranoid schizophrenic."

Well, great. So I knew that my Fifth Step—where you have to read your Fourth Step to your sponsor—had to be at least thirty minutes. My plan was to get a legal pad, sit down in front of the TV, and mute the commercials while I wrote. My sponsor had told me to separate my thinking by seven-year divisions. In other words, write down 0 to 7 years, 8 to 15 years, 16 to 23 years, 24 to 31 years, 32 to 35. So I did that. I labeled the first page 0 to 7, the second page 8 to 15, and so on. Then I sat there while the commercials played silently. I could think of nothing. So I watched fifteen more minutes, muted the commercials, and could think of nothing.

I called my sponsor.

"This isn't working like I had hoped."

"Do you have the TV on?" he inquired.

"Yes, but it's muted when I write."

"How much have you written?" he asked.

"Nothing." Nothing for forty-five minutes.

"Then maybe your way of working isn't working."

He suggested I cut off the TV, kiss the wife and kids goodnight, close the door and start writing. Write the first thing that comes to mind. Write what you're angry about. Write down everything, even if you don't think it's important.

I wrote for twenty-five pages. Legal pad size. Sometimes I wrote on the front and back. Once I started writing, I couldn't stop. I wrote: I'm angry at Melissa for always wanting things, for her rages, for her moods. I wrote that I was angry at my kids because they acted like kids; that I was angry at my boss for firing me; angry at people on the soccer board for bringing me up to an A & D committee; angry at clients who didn't like my work; angry at Melissa's mother.

I couldn't stop writing. A torrent of anger literally flowed through me. I began to remember how my father had lied and raged; I wrote it down. I wrote down the fear I had when my mother slapped my brother. I wrote down how hurt I had been for being thrown off the staff of the high school annual for a trumped up reason.

I wrote down the fear I had when attacked by a bully in seventh grade; the anger I had for being mugged in junior high school. I wrote down how angry I was at the gang of kids I hung out with when I was ten for siding against me when I was fighting another kid. I remembered with fury how one of my best friends stole a paper I had written, copied it word for misspelled word, and as a result I got an "F" for cheating, and he never admitted it.

I remembered things like being in fear of my grandfather because he showed me his razor strap which he said he would beat me with if I needed a beating. This was my first memory of him. The more I wrote, the more I remembered. My preschool days—like when I was four and I tried to tell my mother I needed a lunch for my kindergarten class; she forgot to make it and sent me to school with no food. I had forgotten about that; about how I lied to my teacher and told her I had already eaten while going hungry because my mother wasn't awake to make lunch.

I remembered about how mother couldn't get me to swim meets on time, and I showed up an hour after the race was run. It was like learning about a new person, a new friend, learning all of his secrets, because these were secrets I hadn't admitted to myself. I wrote down how much I hated my nickname, about how most of my life was spent trying not to be the dork my name pegged me as. I remembered feeling like an outsider *early* in life, angry at the way my sixth grade girlfriend dumped me, angry I wasn't cool enough to even be considered. I wrote pages and pages and pages. I wrote how mad I was for being fired years earlier by a scared fifty-five-year-old creative director who saw more of a threat in me than I realized at the time.

I wrote how angry I was at myself for not being a bigger

success, for not making more money, for not being the person I wanted to be. I didn't write that I was angry at Melissa's addiction because I wasn't. But I was furious at her over this "guy" issue. And I wrote down—but nearly erased—that I was angry at my mother for dying.

I took these pages with me to work, and kept adding to the list. People talk about having a flood of memories; I had a torrent. They kept coming. Things I hadn't thought about, people who had really angered me. I couldn't turn the faucet off now that it was stuck open. I'd think of something to add to the 8–15 page sheet; then something would occur to me for the 0–7 page sheet, and on and on and on.

It was a four-day catharsis. I told my wife I was working on a Fourth Step so she would understand the weirdo now sitting across the breakfast table from her (in fact my sponsor strongly suggested I tell my wife what I was doing).

Finally, I called my sponsor and told him I was finished. I couldn't think of any more resentments to write down. "What about sex?" he asked.

"What about it?" I returned.

"Have you written about it?"

"What do I write?"

"Everything," he said. "Write down everything. Tell me about your girlfriends."

Now I am told some people have some truly weird sex stuff. So I actually worried if this part would be too, well, boring. I was assured any evidence of normalcy in my life would be a point in my favor.

So I started writing. And the most astonishing thing was revealed to me. That all my serious girlfriends were addicts or alcoholics or both. That anybody who was "straight" held no interest for me. And while an alcoholic might be momentarily exciting, I could fall in love with just about any blonde drug addict.

My first "real" girlfriend in high school was as perfect

and normal as any mother could want for her son. Cathy was a class beauty, a cheerleader, a straight A student. When I left for college I was unhappy. When I got her letter that she wanted to date the new college guys I was devastated. Until I met Mary. One week later.

Mary was a suicidal alcoholic. Sexually advanced. Mentally unstable. Possessive. Neurotic. I was in love. Her father died of alcoholism around November. She was lost. I was more in love. She was more possessive. I quit hanging around with my friends. I didn't realize just how hooked I had become until December when Cathy called and said she wanted us to get back together. Here she was a freshman beauty queen, Dean's list, campus favorite—I was bored to tears with her.

I knew Mary was trouble but I couldn't help it. She tried to commit suicide several times the next semester. Nothing overt, just walking down the middle of the freeway late at night. Coincidentally, these suicide attempts occurred every time I suggested we start dating other people. But she got stranger and stranger. I felt like I was in the middle of a giant spider web struggling desperately but unable to get away. I'll never forget the night her mother hugged me and said, "Mary told me about your wedding plans." I was eighteen. I was out of my league. Finally the semester ended, and I made a long distance phone call, surrounded by several of my male friends, to break up with her. Very odd.

The next year, I transferred to SMU and met Susan. Very rich, very elegant, daughter of Houston high society. She drank so much that she had to help pay for it. Once again, I was hooked. One weekend we went to Houston to meet her parents and to go to a society ball. I was very impressed with her neighborhood, her mansion, her butler and her parents. They did not have the same reaction to me.

It didn't matter, she whispered to me that Sunday morning as she tried to get in my bed while her parents slept in the next room. I told her if she didn't leave, her father would kill me and my body would never be found. It didn't matter. I loved her more than Mary. However, her father demanded we break up, and she became engaged to a scion of the Ford Motor family. I was heartbroken then. Marriage to her would have been the consummate hell.

Then there was the alcoholic actress, the drunk young Republican, the acid queen hippie, the stoned lifeguard, the alcoholic princess, another brief encounter with high-way-walking Mary. Looking back, I believe it can be stated that by my senior year in college I had discovered a new reality yet to be visited by other mortals. Then I left school and met Melissa, who was clearly the most normal one of the bunch.

The fact is, I had sought out her drug-addict personality, just as she sought out an Al-Anon personality to take care of her. I suppose that's why I was never really resentful of Melissa for being an addict. Indeed, far from being the strangest woman in my life, she was the most normal. It was by God's grace I found her. I was just barely avoiding the real fruitcakes.

Being an addict was something Melissa had a lot of guilt over. More than I can possibly imagine. But I think when I told her I couldn't have fallen in love with her if she wasn't an addict, that may, just may have helped ease some of her pain. Because the fact is, marriage to anyone else *that I would have married,* probably would have killed me.

How did I wind up married to Melissa? It was simple. I had looked for her all my life.

Writing a Fourth Step helped me to see all of this. But there was one more terribly difficult thing I had to do. Step Five.

STEP FIVE. Admitted to God, to ourselves and to another human being the exact nature of our wrongs.

*M*aybe it's an American thing. Maybe it's a man thing. But the hardest thing in the world for a man to do is sit down with some other man—whom you're not paying to listen to you—and tell him just how crazy you really are. To read him your resentments. The big ones. The little ones. To tell him your fears. Your fantasies. Your hurts. To laugh with him and cry with him over the most intensely personal things—things you've never told another human before.

But we have to do it.

Step Five is where a lot of men simply drop out of the program. Their egos—their being men—something won't let them do this step. Maybe it's the fact that it requires—demands—complete honesty. That nothing be held back. Maybe it's the fear that if we let another person know our deepest, darkest secrets, we will be reviled or shamed.

It's hard, but okay, we reason, to tell a psychiatrist who's charging $125 an hour just how neurotic and crazy we are; what bizarre thinking we have, what seemingly horrible things our father had done to us growing up. But another man? Charging nothing? It's one of the most difficult things a man can do. It's also just one of the most important things we have to do. If we're to get better. Become whole. Maybe for the first time.

I was in favor of putting this step off. "I don't know, Bill," I would say. "There's work, then soccer of course, then meetings, then Melissa wants me home." Which was a perfectly good excuse until her recovery. But he was adamant. And frankly, Melissa had already done a Fourth Step, and like any real good Al-Anon, I was going to have the perfect recovery. Certainly better than a drug addict's.

Whatever the reason, I agreed to meet my sponsor at his office and do my Fifth Step, which is simply reading your Fourth Step to another person.

Looking back, I think the biggest roadblock—and I can only speak for men here—is that we're taught to keep secrets. We're taught to be strong, bear up, be a man. Keep problems to yourself. Don't tell anyone how weak you are, where you've failed, what your fears are. This causes all kinds of problems. Not just spiritual. But mental and physical as well.

Looking back at my cluster headaches, it's easy now to see how they were the result of pent-up anger and frustration. Sure, medically I was afflicted with something a doctor could see on an X-ray. But also, I've come to believe those clusters were as much an emotional breakdown as they were physical. Had I been spiritually healthy, I don't believe the headaches would have been as crippling—or would have existed at all.

Then six months after I got out of the hospital—two years before my wife got into recovery—I really got sick. After eating something in Los Angeles, I had diarrhea for a week. When the doctors put me in the hospital, I started throwing up. I threw up for another week. I simply couldn't stop. I got weaker and weaker. The priest came to see me. My father-in-law called to say he was coming into town. Fluid was gathering behind my heart. Doctors and nurses wore yellow space suits around me because they thought I might be infectious. A brilliant doctor—and around the clock prayers—saved my life. I was thirty-five.

On the surface, my life was great. But I had chest pains,

I had been hospitalized twice, I was having panic attacks and crippling headaches. I could no longer digest wheat or milk. I was living on various medications. I couldn't sleep. I was worried sick about money. Yet to an outsider, my wife would have been the sick one because she was addicted to drugs.

All of this, every bit of it, was the result of years of pent-up anger, fears, frustrations. I had swallowed them all, tucked them away, refused to deal with them. And they were beginning to kill me. Literally. Anyone who believes resentment is not a life or death disease is tragically mistaken. It can be an insidious killer—via heart attacks, cluster headaches, mysterious stomach ailments. Or resentment can be a stunningly brutal murderer that simply torments people until they kill themselves. I've seen both.

That's what makes a Fifth Step so important. Yet so many men cannot bring themselves to take this step. So they disappear. And so does any chance of real life-changing happiness.

I know that when I began reading my list to Bill in his office I felt like a fool at first. But that quickly passed. After listening for awhile, he would concur, "That was a rotten thing for him to do." Bill would laugh and I'd laugh with him. He would shake his head and say, "Harry, that's horrible." He would tell me some things from his Fifth Step. I remember choking up—I'm not sure over what. I remember smiling, explaining, but not defending, not exaggerating, not making anything bigger or smaller than it was. And I remember a mystical peace that began to encompass both of us. It was okay telling him these secrets. He didn't judge or condemn or anything like that. He listened, he wept, he laughed.

Then after about five hours, we took all twenty-five pages and put them in a paper shredder. He told me those resentments were gone. That it was indeed now all in the past. That I could go on with my life, and I would be free of them haunting me, terrorizing me.

He instructed me to go home and meditate on the fact I have given all these resentments to God to do with as he wishes. He said God would remove them from me. He told me to pray and meditate for about an hour.

Sure, some of these resentments concerned Melissa. But after reading them aloud to my sponsor, I became aware that most of my resentments, my anger, my fears had nothing to do with her whatsoever. The reality was, most of my anger was with my mother, my father, my bosses, stuff that had happened years ago.

The most amazing thing was that on the way home I felt extraordinarily *alive*. Pumped up. Rejuvenated. As I drove home, more memories began to flood my mind. I dug out my yellow pad and wrote furiously at stoplights. When I got home, I wrote some more. I called Bill and read him the new list, and he said I would probably keep this up for a couple of days. Which I did.

Well, several things happened immediately. In the next four weeks I lost ten pounds. Just gone! I didn't diet, didn't step up my exercise—I just lost weight. People began to comment on how good I looked. I had been taking medicine to control my cluster headaches; I didn't seem to need it anymore. My job, my marriage, my life just began to go smoother. I have no explanation.

I wasn't aware that I was carrying grudges around regarding Melissa, but maybe I was. Free of all my resentments, I could see she was working an outstanding program. She was killing herself to be a good mother and wife. The woman I had loved had returned and I hadn't noticed. Until now.

There's one other thing about a Fourth and Fifth Step for an Al-Anon. One rarely is enough. And sometimes you still have to see a psychiatrist. Several years later, I began having headaches again. Very bad this time. I got back on beta blockers, heart medicine, medicines to control the arteries in my brain. Sitting in my physician's office one afternoon, Charlie looked at me and said, "Harry, you're having cluster headaches, that's for sure. But I also think you're having a major league depression."

Well, I was flabbergasted. I told him that was impossible, that I lived in complete serenity. I said I had done a Fourth Step, and that a "major league depression" was just not possible. I had headaches, for Pete's sake, but my life was fine, so just give me some painkillers.

I called my sponsor. He told me that he thought the doctor was right.

"I've done a Fifth Step," I told him. "Why am I now having a depression?"

"Maybe you need to do another one," my sponsor answered. "Maybe you're not finished."

Clearly, everyone was nuts. I told this to the shrink the next week. I patiently explained I had done a Fourth and Fifth Step, cleared out all the garbage, so I was fine. I just had headaches. My once brilliant doctor needed to get off his duff and get busy finding a cure. Then I started crying. I couldn't stop. And I remember thinking, "What is this?" I was shaking because I was crying so much. The psychiatrist suggested we meet a couple more times.

Why it all was coming down on me then is still a complete mystery to me. My best guess is that working a spiritual program eventually made me come face-to-face with some terrible realities I was living with.

We talked about my mother's death and how it all seemed to be shrouded in secrecy. I didn't know how or why she had died; she just died. Yes, I was sixteen when she died and devastated. The day after the funeral dad had her clothes and jewelry cleared out and we didn't see mom's family *ever* again.

We talked about my father and his addictions and his insanity. After some probing questions, I explained that my dad had married someone half his age, but that that marriage ended in divorce. Then ten years later, he had married big money and had gone entirely off his rocker. I saw my father only about once a year.

We talked about Melissa, and how I felt I wasn't good enough for her. We talked about my career worries, nothing huge, no big insights. But after four meetings with him, I was better. I continued to pray, of course, and continued to meditate. The cloud lifted.

I did my second Fourth and Fifth Steps shortly thereafter. I can't even tell you what I wrote about. I don't remember. But I continued to get better. I had never heard of a shrink being so successful in only four sessions. But I noticed when you've laid the spiritual groundwork, strange things happen. Quickly.

STEP SIX. Were entirely ready to have God remove all these defects of character.

*F*ear. Resentments. Control. Criticism. Honesty. Courage. Massive ego. Selfishness. Judgmentalism. Take all this away and I'd be left with—well, what?

That's why Step Six stresses "entirely ready." But before anybody can change, there has to be willingness to do so. And no one enters Al-Anon because they're just flooded with self-improvement aspirations. Men don't want to change themselves so much as they want to change the alcoholic or addict they're living with. It's this theory that it's we—the "well" ones—who have to change that bothers so many men. Implicit in this step is the rationale that we *need* to be changed.

Why do we have to get rid of our defects? Why do we have to change? The simple reason is this: if we don't change—mentally, spiritually and emotionally—it's quite likely we will leave our recovering wives (or they will leave us), and go find someone sicker.

In Al-Anon, we say there are no victims, only volunteers. We volunteer for the misery that besets us. We may say we hate it. We may openly cry how bad our marriage is, how drunk our wives are, how they spend money like there's no tomorrow, how they have the emotional maturity of a twelve-year-old. It's like living in the Twilight Zone. But the cold reality is that we don't marry someone without knowing about the whole package. Maybe they're not using yet, but they're already drinking more than other women.

Melissa drank a quart of champagne on our wedding night and *didn't get drunk.* I just figured women from Montana could do that.

Men will claim they're stunned that their wives are addicts, but when pressed they will acknowledge that yes, their wives did do coke or weed while they were dating. Yes, their wives have always had some emotional issues. Yes, compulsive spending has always been an issue, but no, they just don't see how they're drawn to that type of woman. Their wives just mysteriously changed overnight from Mother Teresa to the antichrist.

The problem is that my issues with fear, resentments, control, criticism, honesty, courage, humility, selfishness and judgments; my memories of my mother and her death, my father's alcoholism, my childhood all combined to lead me to search out an emotionally unstable personality with a tendency toward drug addiction as the ideal wife.

And Melissa's upbringing in an alcoholic home led her to look for a critical, controlling, judgmental perfectionist as a husband. We both passed up lots of "normal" people trying to find each other. And when we succeeded, we got married.

After almost a year of sobriety, Melissa was working a beautiful program. She was no longer thrilled to have a husband come home and "help" her boil water. She was no longer happy to hear my suggestions on how she might improve herself. She no longer cared to hear my comments, suggestions, hints or criticisms.

The only problem was that I was as hopelessly addicted to criticism as she was to drugs. My criticism could have destroyed our marriage faster than Valium ever could. I think—once again—I got into criticism in an effort to keep Melissa from experiencing pain—the pain of doing something wrong, the pain of not cooking a meal right, not being a "good" mother, not being a good wife, whatever.

A lot of it was also that I expected her to be able to read my mind on everything from sex to money to TV shows. When she failed I criticized her. It wasn't like, "You're the worst wife in the world." It was more subtle, more devastating. It was, "The eggs aren't cooked right." Or, "What is this check for?" Another time, it would be, "Let me adjust the flame on the stove." Or, "Do you not like sex?" I always had an ulterior motive. I wanted something done differently, but rather than say, "I like it this way," I would say, "Why do you have to do it that way?"

I was not well. And I couldn't stop.

I criticized my kids and my wife in a manipulative way. I would point out how they could better themselves. How other people would like them better for what they did better. I thought I was helping. I was killing. And I was no more "entirely ready" to stop than I was entirely ready to stick needles in my eye.

I know how an addict feels when they need to use, because I had that same need to criticize. Something would happen, something stupid. For example, dinner wasn't up to my lofty demands, or the house was dirty, or we had just watched a particularly sad movie she had picked out—anything. Something in me would start in my gut. I'd start breathing real shallow. I'd know she needed correcting, but I'd also know I shouldn't say a word. Then this beast would come alive in my body and I'd fight it down, and it would rise back and I'd be desperately trying to find a way to criticize so that it wouldn't sound like criticism.

I'd try, "Next time let's watch a comedy." Or if I couldn't figure that out, I'd resist the urge to blurt out something, then I'd start literally sweating. I'd be talking to myself, "Don't say a word, please don't say a thing. For once in your life keep your mouth shut!" Then I'd try to catch my breath and failing that, suddenly I would shriek, "Why'd you watch that stupid movie if it was going to make you cry?" or "I told you to put milk in mashed potatoes" and wham! that's it; I would have used!

I was as much an addict as my wife was. There was only one difference. She was clean! In eight or so months Melissa hadn't used. And I was using daily! So clearly I had to stop. If criticism was a drug, it would have killed me. As it was, it was killing my marriage.

Criticism, of course, is linked to control which is linked to fear. I tried to control things because of fear—fear of what would happen if I didn't control things. If I didn't control things, my kids could be kidnapped—or worse, unhappy. They might not make class valedictorian or starting goalie or be popular. My wife might make the wrong decision and wind up in tears. Or pain. Fear that they might be unhappy or hurt or left out is what led me to control things. And leads me today.

(While writing this book, a beautiful, popular high school drill team captain was killed when her boyfriend drove into a tree, vaporizing the car. He was drunk. They both were known drinkers—or as today's liberated parents like to say, "experimenters"—with alcohol. It was a crash over homecoming weekend and it devastated the community. My reaction was simple: I'd control where my fifteen-year-old son goes, whom he goes with, have him home by nine, and so on. I was scared out of my wits. That's how I react when I'm fearful: control.)

Trying to control the uncontrollable was wearing me down. I was beginning to hate myself for criticizing, for feeling the need to criticize, for being literally addicted to criticism. I was like a drug addict: I said I wasn't going to use anymore, I swore I wouldn't, then something would happen and I would feel like using. I'd tell myself I wasn't going to do it, then I'd blurt out some criticism. Then I hated myself for twenty-four hours, made all kinds of feeble apologies, then started the whole charade over. Clearly, this was no way to live. My wife had been clean for months. I couldn't stay clean for eight hours.

Every time I criticized my wife, it was like hitting her. I couldn't just love my kids; I had to correct them. I had to show them how to run faster, throw farther, kick harder. It was always "I love you, but..."

But was I really ready to give up control? What would happen to my company, my family, my life? Sure, sure, I had made the decision to turn my will and my life over to God back at Step Three, but Step Six is there saying, "Look, we know you tried, but now you're going to ask God to finish the job you couldn't. Like give up control. With Step Three you turn everything over to him. Step Six admits that maybe you hung onto something. But now you're ready to give it up.

But was I? If I was entirely ready to give up control, then that would mean my wife might be unhappy. Unhappy enough to leave, unhappy enough to use, unhappy enough to feel pain. It might mean my kids wouldn't have a story-book existence. It might mean I would go totally broke.

And control was certainly not the only defect of character I held onto.

Resentments seemed to accumulate in an invisible brief-case. I had them filed and catalogued, ready to pull out and wave around at the slightest provocation. I could remember one of Melissa's slights of ten years earlier. This resentment thing—in its own way—was almost as devastating as control and criticism. It meant I could never truly forgive anybody for anything. At just the right time, a six-year-old or thirty-year-old resentment could rear its head and make me physically ill. And of course, I had to take it out on somebody. The Fourth Step did a lot for clearing out the conscious resentments. But the act of letting go, consciously not holding onto resentments, that's a Step Six issue. And that's where we lose a lot of men.

I think men are taught as boys to use their anger to get ahead, to come back when their team is down, to motivate them to beat the other guy. I think men are taught that resentments are okay. "Don't get mad, get even," is an expression I heard often. The problem here is that unresolved anger turns into resentments. And I was saddled with a boatload of them by the time I was thirty-five. And I didn't know it. I just had headaches, strange stomach ailments, high blood pressure, mild personality disorders, but only my sponsor could see that I was the angriest man he had ever met. I had no idea.

So what's the risk of losing your resentments, of giving them up? Well, clearly, the biggest risk is, you won't get even. (You'll lose control.) I would never be able to hold this "guy thing" over my wife's head. I would have to not only forgive my boss for firing me, but let go of any "justifiable" anger that would necessitate forgiveness at all. In fact, one of the subtle goals of Al-Anon is simply to teach us not to judge anyone—for anything—and if we don't judge them, we don't have to forgive them. But the spiritual truth in all this is that letting go of resentments—far from being a generous act—is one of the most selfish acts a person can commit.

I'll never forget one Al-Anon meeting, when I was about six months into the program, at which the subject was forgiveness. I was prattling on about my father and how his alcoholism and his marriages and his craziness were simply unforgivable and how maybe he was the reason my head was so screwed up and my stomach continued to torment me. A man named James said to me, "Harry, this stuff is fifteen years old; don't you think it's time to forgive your father?"

I coolly replied, "He doesn't deserve forgiveness."

James looked at me and said, "Maybe not. But don't you?"

Didn't I deserve the peace of mind, the freedom, the release of living a life with no resentments? Didn't I deserve the "letting go" of not continually carrying this anger around? Didn't I deserve a life of happiness, not bitterness? Of course I did. It just didn't occur to me it was within my own power to have all these things by letting go of truly justifiable resentments. By letting go, forgiveness was unnecessary.

Resentments. Fear. Control. Criticism. They were all related. They were all killing me and my marriage. Yes, I realized I wanted to be relieved of these defects. But fear, criticism and control had been so much a part of my life for so long, I really didn't know if such a feat was possible. I remembered a saying that Al-Anon is a program of progress not perfection. Then I read the step again: "...were entirely ready for *God* to remove all these defects of character."

It came back to God. It always does.

STEP SEVEN. Humbly asked Him to remove our shortcomings.

Step Seven is one of those steps I would like to do one time and then be done with the whole thing. I would also like to be able to do it while in the shower, or driving to work, or perhaps between commercials during the NFL Game of the Week. "God, look, I know I'm not perfect, please make me perfect; gotta go, game's starting."

Well, it doesn't work that way. It's also important to note two key words: "humbly" and "him."

So much of recovery is based on prayer. The Third Step prayer. The Seventh Step prayer. The Eleventh Step which is all about prayer. To try and overlook the fact that this program is based on constant communication with God is to miss the whole point. I didn't wake up one morning as this completely deranged husband who had recently been fired and whose wife was being admitted to a treatment center because I was so spiritual. I had to come to terms with who my higher power was, my definition of him and whether or not I could trust him with my life in earlier steps.

Now I had to put my faith to the test: I had to ask him for something. I had to ask him to remove my shortcomings. I had to believe he would do it. That he was anxious to do it. That he was only waiting for me to raise my hand—to call out to him—to do it.

I also had to come to terms with my place in the universe when compared to God. "Humbly" asking him implies a humility, not a sense of "God, you owe me this." But rather, "God, I need your help. I can't do this without you. I can't do this if it isn't your will."

One night, I had a memorable argument with a born-again Christian creative director driving through the streets of L.A. He was screaming at me in the back of a cab that he was filled with humility. I was laughing at his pomposity. Truth was, I didn't know what humility meant. It does not mean hangdog subservience bordering on martyrdom. It does mean knowing one's place in comparison to God's. That he is the creator, we are his creation. That he cares for us, but that our life, our existence, our happiness depend on him.

That's all humility means. Knowing that he's big enough to solve our petty little mundane problems. I recently heard a recovering alcoholic say, "My God's big enough to handle this problem." That is perhaps one of the most reassuring truths in today's world. I came to believe that my God is big enough to handle my career escapades, my house payments, the health and safety of my wife and children. He was also big enough to help me get rid of a few defects.

But I also had to learn my time-frame isn't God's time-frame. What seems like an eternity to me is a second to him. Letting go so God can work on his time-frame and not mine is another lesson in humility. So we are taught not to try and remove everything at once. A selfish, fearful, critical man doesn't usually wake up loving, compassionate and generous overnight. But with God's help, we can work on one defect at a time in increments until it's gone or under control. Not that overnight miracles don't happen. For some they do. If God feels that's what's necessary.

But for most of us, it is rarely just one prayer. And it is rarely only up to God. I prayed to God to be rid of the defect of control and criticism. That was my wish. I desperately wanted it. But the craving didn't just instantly leave me. I had to battle it. Almost immediately after praying to God to be relieved of the addiction to control (this was about eight months or so into the program) my oldest son Sage and his mom got into one of their mind-boggling arguments. He was six. She was thirty-three. And it was hard to tell which was acting the more mature or more childlike.

I had come in late and was eating cereal at the breakfast table when their argument started. Now my tendency had always been to interfere, to tell Sage his mother didn't mean what she said, to tell Melissa that Sage had not meant to hurt her, to act as Solomon in their argument and pass judgment. I would try to get everyone to see the wisdom of my actions—in other words, to control. A perfectly acceptable task of a loving father and husband, which completely undermines the relationship between mother and son.

So the argument started, and I made a point to pick up the cereal box and start reading. The argument got more heated and I began reading the twelve-hour old morning paper. There was a pause in the argument; everyone looked at me. I looked at them and realized this is where I had usually made my presence felt. I immediately began reading the Women's Section.

The argument started up again. I switched to the financials. Voices got higher, then paused again. The combatants looked at me in expectation of interference, and I beat down the tendency to do so. I rather studiously began examining the obits. It went this way for what seemed like a half hour. Rage, pause, rage, pause. I was on my fourth bowl of cereal when a miracle happened. THEY SOLVED IT THEMSELVES. For the first time. Ever. And after we had put Sage to bed, I told Melissa, "You don't know how much I wanted to control that situation."

And she told me, "You don't know how bad we wanted you to."

That's the way most character shortcomings are dealt with. Slowly. Painfully. One step at a time. My sponsor told me that if I ever felt a need to criticize my wife, to call him instead. Rip her apart if I wanted to. Just not to her face.

Well, this proved to be a truly eye-opening experience.

To begin with, no woman returns home from treatment having spent her off days watching Julia Child or reading the *Joy of Cooking*. And one of my worst traits had been to come into the house and adjust the pots on the stove for Melissa, just so dinner would be cooked right. In fact, I would leave work early just to be there in time to "help" her measure ingredients, set the temperature and so on. I knew a thirty-five-year-old woman couldn't serve an edible meal without my guidance. I "helped" her cook dinner for, oh, fifteen years. It never occurred to me she might actually want to cut my hands off for this. Besides, in my mind, dinner was always on the verge of going to hell if I didn't "help." I tried to convey the situation to my sponsor, that our family's nightly nutrition depended upon my generous New Age acceptance of a man's place in the kitchen. He was unimpressed.

"Call me the next time you want to interfere," he said.

"I'm not interfering," I told him. "I am helping." "There may be some slight control issues here," I acknowledged, "but my family's dinner depends upon them."

"Call me," he repeated.

So that night I came home and dinner had the look and smell of disaster. I left the controls alone. The instant potatoes were too runny. The beans weren't cooked enough. There wasn't enough meat. It all looked wrong to me.

"Honey," I said pleasantly, "I need to make a phone call."

I went upstairs and called my sponsor.

"She can't boil water," I told him.

"Good," he said. "Proves she's going to meetings."

"I mean, dinner is going to be terrible," I said. I went on from there. I complained. I moaned. I criticized. I bitched about my day. Then I went downstairs and ate a truly mediocre meal.

"You hate dinner," she said.

"Loved it," I lied.

"It tasted terrible," she said. She blinked back tears. Her eyes looked tired, her face drawn. The thought occurred to me that she must have put in a tough day. And I thanked God I hadn't said a word. I could see she was trying. She expected me to criticize. Probably wanted me to. Her psyche probably felt she deserved it. It was a trap I had walked into many, many times.

"It was fine," I insisted. I kept on. "And I know for fifteen years I've tried to control how you cook dinner, and I know I've been wrong. I do it unconsciously. The problem is me, not you. And I don't even know when I do it."

Incredulous, she wiped her mouth with her napkin.

"So I'm going to stay out of the kitchen from now on, unless you invite me in. And if I start adjusting temperatures and adding ingredients again, just tell me to leave."

Ten years later, my boys and I don't like anybody else's cooking except hers. Somehow, she became a great cook without my help. In fact, it was when I quit helping that she actually began to enjoy it. Do I ever slip up when I'm in the kitchen and start adjusting ingredients? Of course. But now, I quickly realize what I'm doing and back off. Or if it's a dish she's cooking just for me, like rice, which I like a certain way—she doesn't get mad when I make it like I like it. She realizes I'm still mentally ill with no immediate hope for recovery, and doesn't take it personally. But overall, it's simply healthier for me to help with the dishes rather than the meal.

And that's pretty much how I had to handle all my criticism and control issues. Call my sponsor, whine about it for a half hour, then come downstairs and not say a thing to my wife about my distress. And ACT HAPPY. Not like a martyr. I have to keep remembering that nothing happens in God's world by mistake. I'm not fit to judge anyone but myself, and even then I have to be careful.

I quit coaching soccer and both my sons flourished. They wound up with much better coaches than I ever was. And it was a relief to lean back and watch them play and just cheer for them rather than correct them, because I had put the weight of their team on their shoulders.

I quit trying to control my wife's relationship with her mother (though this was one area where she was comfortable with my interference), and they now have a working relationship. And arguably, I have the best relationship with my mother-in-law of any of her children, because I no longer judge her by my wife's definition of her, but by the way she and I interact.

I quit criticizing my wife for her spending and instead, we worked out a formula for how much money she needed every week for groceries, servants, and so on. I don't care where that money goes, and she doesn't tell me, though most of it, I suspect, goes to feed our boys. But the point is, that's her money, she's responsible for it, and it's not my concern. And it's one less thing for me to complain about.

I don't attempt to control where my wife goes. Quite often on Sundays, I'll go to church with the boys and she goes to her meetings. Instead of trying to get her to come to church with me, I thank God she loves herself and us enough to go to those meetings. But I know men who would insist that their recovering wives go to church with them, if for nothing else but appearance's sake.

I turned my family's health and safety over to God. And I continue to do so every morning. I still worry about my family and probably will forever. But I know there is a force in the world bigger than I who takes care of them. I no longer have panic attacks that lead me rushing to the hospital for an electrocardiogram.

I battle the fear of financial insecurity daily, though in my morning prayers, I can truthfully turn over our finances to God. And I no longer judge my career by the advancement or failures of others. I've even come to believe that God will always take extraordinary care of us, but never let us get too comfortable, for no other reason but that I won't make money my higher power again. God has never let me down.

I'm free of living with resentments today. Not that I don't get mad at people, not that I don't temporarily let my anger or resentments get the best of me. But I know I now have a choice as to whether or not I want to stay mad, have conversations in my head, plot revenge, make them my higher power.

The method the program teaches us for dealing with resentments is one that flies in the face of everything we're taught as men. Instead of acting tough and seeking revenge, we're taught that not only do we have to pray to God to be free of a resentment, we have to also pray to God *for that individual.* Jesus often talked about praying for our enemies, and now I understand what he was talking about.

My sponsor told me I had to pray for anyone I held a resentment against. Over the years I've had to pray for my father, my ex-boss, my mother-in-law, people who were trying to throw me off the soccer association board, clients who had fired me, employees whom I had to fire, kids who were mean to mine, women who hated my wife, anyone I was mad at. This is tough. Having to get on your knees and say, "God, I know I'm lying; you know I'm lying; but please grant Ed, jerk that he is, every emotional, physical, financial and spiritual prayer that he wants." For thirty days, I had to say that prayer about anyone who had wronged me.

Strange, spiritual and mystical things happen when you pray for your enemies. Even though God knows you're lying, somewhere during the third week, your hate dissipates. It is simply impossible to pray for someone you hate, so if you continue to do so, your hate goes away. And after the fourth week, not only do you stop hating that person, invariably your relationship becomes stronger. Go figure.

The Seventh Step is instrumental in cleaning house. But as my sponsor told me one night, I wasn't through. Now it was time to deal with people's resentments toward me. It was time to move on to the Eighth Step.

STEP EIGHT. Made a list of all persons we had harmed, and became willing to make amends to them all.

O ne of the hardest things for me to vocalize are the words, "my fault." My lips refuse to make the right shape. I start stammering and stuttering. In order to avoid this seemingly easy task, I simply try to be right all the time. Never make a mistake. A slip-up. Or an error. Always be right. And of course, the problem with always trying to be right is what happens when you are clearly, totally, inarguably in the wrong. When you've screwed up.

Quite often, it's rock-hard, ironclad, intractable denial.

I remember one very successful man telling me that what drove him was the fear of making a mistake. That fear drove him to financial heights. He had a beautiful wife, beautiful children, a beautiful home, a "hot" company—until his inability to admit he could be wrong plummeted him to financial ruin. He also lost his marriage, his home and his best friend.

Most men seem to believe that to admit being wrong is to admit to a fatal flaw. That it is better to defend to the death an insane action rather than just apologize and get on with life. I think it probably has to with the perceived weakness in making an apology. Saying "I'm sorry." Asking forgiveness. Men don't do this very well at all.

But this is the whole point in the Eighth and Ninth Steps: Admit we were wrong. Ask to be forgiven. Use those words: "Will you forgive me?"

Seeking forgiveness is perhaps the most difficult part of a spiritual journey. In the New Testament, Jesus would usually first forgive the sins of a critically ill person who was brought to him for healing. This, of course, would totally baffle the ill one and his friends. Years and years after first reading these passages, I finally get it. Jesus knew all sickness was based on a spiritual sickness. He couldn't cure the body until he had first treated the soul.

That's the situation I found myself in. Making a list of the people I had harmed. Starting with my wife.

To do an Eighth Step requires a fearless assessment of the situation and our part in it. The role we played. The damage we are responsible for. She may be the drug addict but I owed her more than an apology, I needed to make amends. I needed to ask her forgiveness for criticizing her every move, and finding fault in every situation. In a bizarre attempt to look out for her own good, I was the one who was causing the most harm. It took me nine months or so to see I was the demanding one, the hard-to-please one, the insistent one, the stingy one, the rigid one, the inflexible one, the cold one.

The insane one.

I was the one who always thought dinner needed to be cooked longer. The kitchen cleaned better. The kids entertained more. I was the one who thought Melissa incapable of picking her own friends, managing her mother, dealing with crises. I was the one who could never relax, never take it easy, never enjoy the moment. If it was the weekend I had to be mowing the yard. If I wasn't mowing the yard, I was pulling weeds. And if I wasn't pulling weeds, I was cleaning the garage. I was never content, never satisfied. Since I was hardly happy with my own life, how could I possibly be happy with hers? So I made her happiness the basis for my happiness and because she wasn't happy, I was frustrated. Angry. Scared.

Very, very scared.

Scared she wouldn't be happy. Scared she would leave. Scared she would criticize me, hold me accountable for her happiness. Scared I couldn't measure up. In my desperate attempt to force her to be happy, to see the error of her ways, and by my continually trying to change her, I was killing her. And us.

Then there were our children, especially our older child, Sage, whose only sin was being unable to perform up to a standard on a soccer field that was set by a deranged father.

So Melissa was number one. Making amends to her would go a long way toward healing our marriage. Making amends to my oldest son was something I had to do even though he was only six. My younger son at the time was four, so really the only thing I could do for him was determine not to be as insane as in the past. But there were other amends to be made, because my sponsor assured me I couldn't be sane and rational unless I had totally and completely cleaned up my side of the street.

I had made a short list. My ex-boss, my mother-in-law, my father.

"How do I know whom I should make amends to?" I asked him. "I mean, I'm in advertising, so I could spend the rest of my life apologizing to people."

He told me the ultimate test was whether or not I could be in the same room with someone. "If you're not comfortable with that person in the room with you, you need to make amends."

"Well, it could be he's the one who owes me amends," I replied. "It could all be his fault. Like my boss. He fired me. Why should I make amends to him?"

"Why do you ask?" Bill inquired. "Obviously, it's on your mind. If you didn't do anything, why would you be uncomfortable with him in the room?"

(This is the problem men have with the Eighth and Ninth Steps. They fly in the face of everything we have learned since childhood. They tell us that *justified* anger is wrong. My wife was the drug addict and I'm the one making amends. My boss fired me, and I'm making the amends. All because I let their actions make me act resentful and insane.)

Normal people don't have to do these things, I frequently told my sponsor.

"You're not normal," he continually assured me.

"What about your boss?" he persisted. "It sounds to me like you subconsciously believe you owe him amends."

"I don't know," I sighed. "I said some things when it was all over with, some things that got published in a magazine, some things that might have hurt his feelings."

"What do you care?" my sponsor asked. "He fired you."

I remember sitting there for a few minutes. Thinking. "He was good to me," I said quietly. "Maybe I deserved it."

"Maybe you owe him amends," my sponsor said.

Next on my list was my mother-in-law. Let's just say her relationship with her daughter—my wife—was just about everything a dysfunctional mother and daughter relationship could be. She could be hysterical, demanding, and frightening one moment, and morbidly depressed and sad the next. But this was all information I was getting from my wife. Her impressions, not mine. Years earlier I had thrown her mother out of our apartment for drinking. But truthfully, since then she had joined AA, and has become one of the true leaders in her community. Her life has impacted more people than I will ever know.

What I had to separate was Melissa's issues from my issues. Her mother wasn't my issue. In fact, I was quite proud of her mother's accomplishments, though I never told her. But when Melissa was in the throes of her fears about her mom, I was the one who intervened. Who would not let her mother talk to her? Who would coolly insert himself in all their affairs? Who judged how long Melissa should stay at her mom's? Who decided when it was the right time for Melissa to even visit her mom? I would tell Melissa what to say on the phone and in person, what to agree to and not agree to. I would condemn her, rail about her (which sometimes sparked a mystifying argument with my wife, who would say I was being too mean about her mom, when all I was doing was protecting her).

Her mother filled Melissa with fear, and being Melissa's god, I protected her from her mom. Yet in all of our years of marriage, her mother never did anything evil to me, never said anything bad about me, never acted unfriendly to me. She just acted like a mother-in-law trying desperately to save a faltering relationship with her daughter. In fact, I had even come to believe that as a grandmother to our two boys, she was terrific. I came to understand Melissa's mother was Melissa's problem, not mine. And even though her mother sometimes made her afraid, it was still *not my problem*. Her mother was nothing but nice and kind to me and our boys.

"You owe her amends," my sponsor agreed.

Then there was my brother. "Why him?" my sponsor asked.

"Because I can see how much my younger son adores his brother, who treats him like dirt," I replied. "And Sage is a better big brother than I ever was. If Mark loved me as much as Field loves Sage, and I treated him that way, I have to make amends. For being a bastard."

Field would wake up in the morning and his first question was always "Where's Sage?" He would wake up after a nap and ask, "Where's Sage?" He was happy just to be in his brother's presence, although he would be ridiculed, told what to do and sometimes pounded by boys twice his size. But he kept coming back for more. It broke my heart to think I did the same thing, only worse. I remembered Mark was the one who would loan me money in college, not my father, and I never even paid him back. Mark and I had grown closer over the years since college, but I had never told him how fond I was of him.

"Make amends," my sponsor agreed.

Then finally on my list was my father.

"Why him?" my sponsor asked. "What did you do?"

"Well," I answered thoughtfully, "nothing."

And that's a fact. I had done nothing to make amends for. After our mother's death, my brother, sister and I attempted to rally around him. But when I thought about it, I realized he's the one who married a woman almost half his age seven months later. He's the one who threw my sister out of the house (upon his wife's request) when she was still in high school. He's the one who would stagger into my brother's room late at night and read him his will, telling him how rich we were all going to be when he died.

He's the one who let his wife talk him into moving out of our family home into a bigger home because of my deceased mother's "presence." Then out of that home into a smaller home. Then out of that home into an apartment. Then my young stepmother moved out, divorced him, and got almost everything he had.

He's the one who then began dating and eventually married a rich, alcoholic widow. He's the one who would drunkenly call to invite my wife and me over for dinner and when we showed up at the door had forgotten all about the invitation. He's the one who didn't want to see me for two years because I turned down his sixteen-year-old stepson's invitation to spend the night on their yacht when I learned there would be marijuana, not to mention some serious high school sex onboard. My delinquent stepbrother whined that I'd hurt his feelings; I had messed up his party.

My father was the one who took so many pills even his third wife, in her drunken stupor, called me in a panic one night to come take him to the hospital after he over-dosed. He's the one I took to the hospital when he fell down his steps at eleven P.M. when, in a drunken fog, he decided to go jogging in a snowstorm. He's the one who was accused of stealing from his company and lost his regional manager's job. He's the one who had me uninvit-ed from a family reunion because I didn't have the money to lend him for a new car. The fact was, I felt I didn't owe him a thing. Which for an Al-Anon is a very uncomfort-able position.

"I don't know," I told my sponsor. "But I feel guilty."

"That's why you're in Al-Anon," he said. "But you've done nothing. Can you just accept the fact your father is simply an alcoholic? If anything, he owes you a few amends."

And that's why we need sponsors. Men are so reluctant to get them, but sponsors can help us find the trees through the forest. We talked about several other people I needed to make amends to. I revealed secrets I had never told anyone about. Then there was one last person I need-ed to make amends to, I said. My mother.

"What did you do?" he asked, knowing the obvious problem.

"It just feels like I should," I lied.

"Well, you can always just talk to her during your medi-tations and prayers."

"Sure," I told him. "I can do that."

We parted shortly thereafter. I had my list of amends to make. I went to an Al-Anon meeting, talked to several guys after the meeting, then went home, and when every-one was in bed, I stole downstairs. I kept the light off, sat in the chair, got real still. I closed my eyes. And waited.

"Mom," I finally said. "I don't remember ever telling you I love you. And I do. Still. And I miss you."

For the first time, since she died, my eyes teared up.

***STEP NINE.* Made direct amends to such people wherever possible, except when to do so would injure them or others.**

Step Nine is like Step Five: I could just think of all kinds of reasons not to do it. It's an action step. It requires movement, motivation, and most of all it requires a leap of faith—faith that you can confront this person you've harmed, and that you can say the right thing. It's faith that they won't hate you forever. For a man, the difficulty is that you have to lay aside your masculinity and toughness. You're all but inviting criticism, a tongue-lashing. You're admitting you're wrong. You're admitting fault. This is something we Al-Anons don't do well.

As I've said before, the program is—on the face of it—an odd way to live. Pray for your enemies. Let go of things you've always tried to control. If you're having a problem with some person, look at yourself first. Turn your health and finances over to God. And of course, make amends to your wife—the drug addict.

Very odd. But also absolutely essential—to you, to your marriage, to your spiritual well-being. Yet perhaps the most extraordinary thing was that by now I could see my fault in this whole matter. I could see how I was driving her crazy, how I was criticizing, controlling, manipulating, demeaning—how I was destroying her.

I was sincerely aghast; I had no idea how it had gotten so out of hand. And even though the Al-Anon creed is that "You can't cause it, you can't control it, you can't cure it," the fact is, I would have had to take nine Valiums a day also just to live with me. I couldn't see my part in the whole deal back when Melissa got out of treatment. Then I just saw a shaking, quivering drug addict who could never be happy with life, no matter what I bought her.

But now, the blinders were off, the harsh light of reality was setting in. And Melissa had been clean for ten or so months, and I was still having slips. I was still criticizing. Not often, but enough to make me sick of me. I realized that, if criticism was as dangerous for the user as Valium, I would be dead. My wife was clean; I was still sick.

I realized that making proper amends after fourteen years of mental cruelty was going to involve a bit more than leaning over the pot roast one night and quipping, "If you're still mad about all that criticism, hey, I'm sorry."

In fact, I was told to tell her the truth. Tell her I knew what I had done, everything that I remember, that I am now aware of all the criticism and controlling I had subjected her to, that I never set out to be that kind of husband but I realize I had turned into that kind of husband.

"If she gets mad, let her," my sponsor said. "If she wants to yell and scream, let her. Don't defend yourself, don't justify, don't excuse. Remember, you're the one at issue here. But it's been my experience she won't. Melissa will handle it fine." He gave me one more piece of advice. "You might want to pray before you make amends. Ask God to give you the words to say."

Okay. I believed God would do that. Now all I had to do was get the soccer teams coached, eat dinner, play some more with the boys, read to them, say prayers, and by 8:15 have them in bed.

"Let's go downstairs," I told Melissa. "I need to talk to you." As we walked downstairs, I prayed that God would do the talking, and Melissa and I both would listen.

I sat on the couch, she sat on the chair. And that's really

all I remember. I know I told her I knew I had been in the wrong, that my sickness was worse than hers because I couldn't stop. I explained that I loved her the way she was no matter what I said or implied; that I was addicted to criticism and I was trying desperately to stop with limited success. But I don't remember the exact conversation anymore—the specific wrongs, the names, dates and places—because a Ninth Step takes away those memories. But I do remember asking her, "Will you forgive me?"

Those words are important. The words "I'm sorry," are significant only if they are attached to the plea, "Will you forgive me?" or "Please forgive me." "I'm sorry," implies a regret for something. "Will you forgive me?" says I have done something terrible to you; it suggests that the person who has been harmed has an alternative to forgiving you. And it underscores that you—the Al-Anon always in control—are handing over your redemption to another person. It is very spiritual. It is very powerful.

It never fails.

I remember she cried, I cried, we hugged. I remember it took about ten or fifteen minutes because I had a lot to make amends for. It wasn't the defining point in our recovery because I truly believe that had come earlier. But our recovery could not have gone much further if I had not made amends and she had not forgiven me. That's the mystery about the Ninth Step: it's a two-way street—you ask and she responds. Melissa did have an option. She could have reminded me of all the terrible things I did that I had forgotten. She could have said, "Next time I'm out the door." She didn't do any of that. She forgave. It was spiritual. It was mystical. It was wonderful.

I felt as if a boulder had been lifted off my shoulders. All the guilt, the regret, the self-anger I had was gone—because she forgave me. I resolved to work harder than ever at not criticizing. Later that night during my evening prayers, it occurred to me God had indeed put the words in my mouth, words I never could have thought of, said or fathomed.

"Maybe," I thought later, "he'll help with my mother-in-law."

He did. Several days later I called her and told her I wanted to come by for a second. She was stunned. In all the years I'd known her, I had never gone over to her house alone.

But over coffee I told her I was not proud of my actions. Again I don't remember the words, but essentially it was that I knew I had treated her terribly and that I had come between her and her daughter, that I had made her feel unwelcome and I was very sorry. Would she forgive me?

God was clearly working overtime that day.

She was both amazed and gracious, then actually asked for forgiveness for *her actions!* And since that day, our relationship has been extraordinary. I can see that she's a wonderful grandmother; I can see the impact she's had on the community. I can see things I never saw before: her courage in many areas, a sincere spiritual side, and to my astonishment, a generosity I simply had never perceived.

Is she a saint? Heavens, no. She's a mother-in-law whose temper has been known to melt rock. But our relationship is healed. How she deals with the rest of the world is not my problem.

Time to move on to my brother. This was difficult, because he really held no resentments against me. So he was utterly clueless when I called him up one evening—1300 miles away—and began talking to him about the dynamics between big brothers and little brothers, about my sons, about him and me, about all the kindnesses he had shown me growing up.

I apologized for never paying him back the money he loaned me and in words I don't remember, asked his forgiveness. It was the first time—ever—I told him I loved him. He told me he loved me. It was as extraordinary a moment as the amends to my wife. Making amends to my brother opened the door to a relationship as wonderful and enlightening as I have in my marriage, and led to some extraordinary revelations. God clearly was still at work.

Then there was the issue of seeking amends from my ex-boss, the guy who had fired me. To say I had been devastated eleven months earlier would be to underestimate the impact. We had been together eight years, five at his company. I was completely loyal, though frustrated I didn't have as much *control* as I wanted (surprise, surprise). I could trace my wife's rapid decline to the day I was fired (one month later she was in the hospital—seven weeks later she was in treatment) and couldn't fathom why this had all happened.

Shortly after I opened my own company I was interviewed by a friendly reporter for an industry magazine who asked why I had left my old company and defiantly I replied, "I was fired." As I had been an award-winning writer, I knew the message this would send about his agency—and it did. Eleven months later though, I could see some things I couldn't before. It was time I moved on.

Now, for eleven months, I had my own company. My former boss had been quite generous with me in the past, when I had been critically ill and not really of much value to him for about six months. He had actually bought me a Mercedes. And I left his company with one month's salary and a $25,000 pension, so I could actually afford to go into business for myself. Most remarkably, if he had not fired me, Melissa would probably have died.

By then she had been hooked on Valium and other painkillers for at least two years and slowly, very slowly, was sinking. This crisis catapulted her into the hospital with severe headaches, where they first took her off

Valium, which eventually landed her in the treatment center.

I first prayed for God to give me the words. Then I called my former boss and asked if I could stop by for a few minutes. I'm sure he was puzzled. I prayed again when I pulled up in the parking lot. "Why are you doing this?" I asked myself. "I mean, who the flip cares if we are friends again?"

Frankly, I didn't know why I was there, except that my sponsor had told me I should do it.

Again, it was remarkable. I didn't ask him why he fired me or rehash all the great things I had done for him. It was my amend, not his. I simply said I regretted saying specific things in the article. I said that he had shown me a lot of kindness that I would never forget, and asked if he would forgive me. He said there was no need, because he probably would have said even more if he'd been the one interviewed.

We shook hands and parted as friends. So much so that some seven years later, when a group of his "trusted" employees filed suit in a federal court charging violations of a pension/profit-sharing plan and invited me into their lawsuit, believing I had a huge axe to grind, they were mystified when I declined. He was my friend, though I hadn't seen him in awhile and he had fallen upon difficult times. And friends don't sue friends.

That's the way making amends works. They are freeing, exhilarating, inspiring and emotional. They provoke such a rush that you're tempted to make amends to the postman, to the telephone operator, to anyone in your path. But I wasn't doing this for the rush of it all; I was doing this for the spirituality of it .

And there were some amends I couldn't make. The step says, "...made direct amends wherever possible, except when to do so *would injure them or others.*" Making some amends would hurt the other person, so while it would free you, it could enslave them. For those, I was told it was best to make living amends, to just try and love that person a little more and not bring up the past. Not if it would hurt them.

It's one more thing about this program that's confounding, but sometimes recovery is *not* being able to say you're sorry.

STEP TEN. Continued to take personal inventory and when we were wrong promptly admitted it.

*T*he steps are in order for a reason—because you're not ready to do Step Three—to turn your will and your life over to God—until you've bought into the theory that you're as crazy as a bedbug. If things have been going just swell, why bother to turn your will and life over to God to screw everything up?

Step Ten is like that. We're not ready to *continue* to take personal inventory until we've actually done it once. Until we have made a list of our defects. Until we have made a list of amends we need to make. Until we have gone down that list faithfully making those amends. Until we have cleaned up our house, and seen the miracles—only then can we say that we will continue to take personal inventory.

Step Ten is a great relief. Because it means I don't have to be perfect. It concedes I might slip back into control; I might actually criticize. It also acknowledges that Melissa won't be perfect either. That she may rage again; that she may tell me I'm not a good husband again. Step Ten is for the humanness in us all. It says we're going to make mistakes—and it tells us what to do about it: continue to take personal inventory and when we're wrong, promptly admit it.

Personal inventory is just that—an inventory of how we did that day. Or that hour. Or in that last argument. Step Ten has taught me not to let things fester. Before recovery, Melissa could say something—anything—and I would file it away for future torture. To torture me or torture her, it didn't really matter, because rarely was I living in the present anyway. She may say something quite innocently that I may not be well enough to shrug off. The Old Harry would have either exploded—I did that before—or waited until I could embellish it and wave it around it her as proof of her misdeeds. Today, if something's bothering me I ask her about it—not as a confrontation, not in an accusatory way. I just check it out.

And quite often, it's in my own mind.

But the point is, I don't wait. I deal with it immediately.

However, she's human too. She might be in a bad place. Step Ten says that if I want to take issue with something she's said, *do it now.* Talk about it now. Work it out now. Forgive now.

It also says if I've been short, cruel, impatient, unkind—that I shouldn't wait. I need to make amends now. If I've been controlling, make amends now. If I've been selfish, and I just saw the light, deal with it now. Step Ten is maybe one of the greatest tools to use in building a harmonious marriage. It means you won't go to bed without setting things right tonight; it means if you've said something, done something, forgotten to do something—don't wait, don't hesitate, make amends now. If you screw up, deal with it and move on.

"Continue to take personal inventory," means that we never stop looking at ourselves. We never stop going to meetings. We never stop praying and meditating. We never stop reading. Step Ten reminds us this is a lifelong program, just as Melissa's sobriety, our sanity, our marriage, our recovery is a lifelong program.

And the fact of the matter is, as you begin to live this program every day, always looking at yourself, always trying to grow, strange things happen. Answers come.

After three or so years in the program, I had even gotten my brother to a couple of meetings when he was in town. He was having some very difficult marriage problems, compounded by the fact that his wife was at the time slowly sinking into a debilitating depression. This depression eventually turned into a truly nightmarish multiple personality disorder that required both of them to seek therapy.

"It makes perfect sense to me," I told him one day on the phone. "I marry a drug addict and you marry eighty-four people all at once."

"I think it has something to do with mom," he said out of the blue.

"Well obviously," I replied, "it has something to do with mom. But who knows what? She wasn't a drug addict. I don't remember her ever being anyone but mom."

"Don't you ever want to know why she died?" Mark persisted. "My psychiatrist says there has to be more to it than she just died."

"I don't know, Mark; you know what I know. Her pancreas exploded. She died."

He wasn't through. "Don't you ever wonder why we never saw her family again? Why we never saw her mother or her sisters or her brother ever again? That's not normal! Those were our aunts, uncles and grandmother."

He wasn't going to let up. "What do you remember before the age of fifteen?"

"Nothing," I said. "I've never been able to remember anything. I barely remember my bedroom, names, classmates, activities—it was all fog. I never really talked about it. I just wrote it off to not paying attention."

"Same with me," he said excitedly. "You don't remember anything. I don't remember anything. Why don't we remember a goddamn thing?"

"I don't know" I said. "I always just thought I had a bad memory."

We compared notes. We lived in an upper middle class home. Dad was a corporate man; he sold pharmaceuticals and he was very good. Indeed he rose to regional manager. Mom was mom. We didn't remember anything much more about her, except for the fact she was always sick the last two years of her life. Her hands would cramp up.

She and dad would sometimes have screaming fights. I remember as a little boy listening to their fights in a darkened hall, absolutely terrified. We never really saw mom drink. For that matter we never really saw dad drink heavily when we were growing up. But she was sick a lot. Sometimes her medicine made her sick. And a few months before mom died she had gone to the Mayo Clinic where they found her to have major problems with her liver. But didn't know why.

"There's more to it," my brother declared. "And my shrink is going to help me find out."

"Stay in touch," I replied.

Seven days later he called me. The next fifteen minutes would change our lives.

"Do you know mom drank?" he asked.

"No," I replied, flabbergasted. "Where did you get that idea?"

"Don't you remember mom used to keep liquor under her bed so we wouldn't see her drink?" he asked.

"Mark, I honest to God have no memory of that."

"I remember that," he said. "You do, too."

I began fighting desperately for my mothers's honor. "I never saw a bottle. I never saw her drink. I never even smelled alcohol on her."

"She kept bottles under the bed. We found bottles there the day she was taken to the hospital. I remember."

"Mark, I just don't remember."

"Why did she go to the New York clinic?" he fired back.

I racked my brain. "I don't know," I sighed.

"What did they find?" he demanded.

"Nothing." I said. "They found nothing."

"What was wrong with mom's hands?" He wouldn't let up.

"They would cramp up," I almost shouted.

"Why?" he demanded. "There had to be a reason!"

"I don't know," I said angrily. "That was part of her sickness."

"What did she do during the day?" he said, very quietly.

"Nothing." I said. "She did nothing. She slept!"

"Dear God," I whispered. "She slept."

In a flash, thirty years of lies, half-truths and family secrets began melting away. Over the phone we pieced together a picture of our mother that for some unfathomable reason had been blacked out. Her hands had not been cramping; she was having withdrawal symptoms. I had watched Melissa's hands do the same thing. Mom's pills weren't for her sickness; they *were* her sickness.

Her husband was a regional manager of a pharmaceutical company, for God's sake. He believed in pills. Every doctor in Dallas knew him as did every pharmacist. Dad had easier access to uppers, downers, sedatives, sleeping pills than a bartender does to alcohol. Whenever mom tried to quit, she would go into convulsions, hallucinations and rages. Mom was an addict, pure and simple. And thirty years ago, no doctor or clinic, not even the famed Mayo Clinic, knew what drug addiction was. They just said her liver was very damaged, but they didn't know why.

Somehow we stared into each other's souls across 1300 miles.

"I know what happened that night," I said quietly. "Dad and Mom had a fight. Mom reached over, took a handful of something, chased it with the alcohol under her bed and waited. She killed herself."

Mark was almost crying on the other end of the line.

"That's why her family was mad at dad, why we never saw them again, why dad got rid of everything mom owned the day after the funeral, why nobody talked about her. Ever again."

"And why dad is now an alcoholic and drug addict," I said.

I knew we were right. He knew we were right. To check it out, I made a rare phone call to my father. I was beyond angry that for thirty years he would keep a secret like this from us. I was incredulous.

When dad answered the phone, I got straight to the point. "Let me tell you what happened the night mom died," I started the conversation. He was silent for about ten seconds.

"Okay."

"Mom was an addict when nobody knew what drug addiction was. You were her supplier but didn't know what drug addiction was. You guys had a fight. And mom—for whatever reason—took a handful of pills and washed it down with liquor. You didn't know anything happened till early that morning when she went into convulsions and you took her to the hospital."

Silence.

"She killed herself, didn't she?"

He quietly said, "Right before she died, son, she woke up in the hospital and took my hand and said, 'I didn't mean to do it.'"

"Why didn't you ever tell us, dad? It's only been thirty goddamn years. Didn't you think it might be relevant? Were you and your family so embarrassed your wife committed suicide you just decided not to tell us? Ever?"

He didn't have an answer. He hasn't had one in awhile.

All this time I had blamed God for my mother's death. I had even said, "God has never let me down except once," and now I finally realized he had not let me down even then. Mom had killed herself, period. I began to understand my fears of Melissa leaving or dying; my thinking there was always something more I could do to make her happy, my kids happy, not feel pain, not die—because God had been known to drop the ball—and now I realized he had never dropped the ball. In fact he had taken pretty amazing care of some pretty damaged kids who grew up with a lie.

Later, I went to my mother's grave and wept for her, really for the first time since she died. Thirty years of holding everything in came rushing out. "Jesus, mom," I said aloud, standing there crying and feeling the grief and loss of thirty years ago.

I cried some more. I settled down. "I'm not mad at you; I'm not angry; I just wish it could've been different."

I remember bending down at her grave marker. "You didn't even know what was happening. You didn't have a clue." I looked at her grave a little while longer, dried my eyes and said, "By the way, you'd love Melissa. She's just like you."

Finally, it was over.

I went home and hugged my wife very tight that night.

STEP ELEVEN. Sought through prayer and meditation to improve our conscious contact with God *as we understood Him,* praying only for knowledge of His will for us and the power to carry that out.

I cheated on this step.

I was trying to make conscious contact with God from my first day in the program. I suggest you do, too.

The Third Step says we turn our will and our lives over to the care of God as we understand him. Fine and good. So what happens now? Suppose he wants us to forgive our wife rather than keep praying for him to change her? More astonishing, suppose he wants *us* to ask our wife for forgiveness rather than ask him to get her to see the light? How can we hear him? How can we understand him? That's the purpose of Step Eleven.

Step Three says to put God in charge. Step Eleven says stay in touch.

There's also the real spiritual truth that while most people wait until emergencies happen to frantically make conscious contact with God, those who practice Step Eleven faithfully seem to avoid those emergencies. Because they've been listening to God. Every day.

It's like waiting till you're drowning to learn to swim.

Step Eleven is the difference between spirituality and religion. People can show up at church every Sunday, throw their money in the plate, have a cracker and some wine, go home and scream at the wife, the kids, drink till they're unconscious, secure in their religion and wondering why their life is going to hell. Or, a person can actually sit down in front of God—which is very uncomfortable—and very privately listen. And pray. And meditate. And do this daily. There are no awards for this, no record of church attendance—yet you'll attain a serenity you may have never known before.

The first thing to understand about keeping a conscious contact with God is that it involves effort. Giving up something. In fact, everything regarding God generally involves something we don't want to do. So just accept the fact that you may have to give up sleeping late, or seeing "The Late Show," or doing something that you may enjoy doing.

God wants you praying.

Second, there's the issue of where to meditate and pray. Some men look me straight in the eye and say they pray and meditate in the morning while driving to work which, of course, is impossible. So let's just get some ground rules down about prayer and meditation. Praying in your car doesn't count, even though most reasonable people generally utter a prayer or two every time they get into their automobile these days.

But Step Eleven isn't like that. It's a special, if sometimes inconvenient, time that is between me and my God.

Praying in the shower doesn't count.

Praying while exercising doesn't count.

Praying during commercials doesn't count.

Praying in your office counts only if the door is closed, everyone is gone, and you don't mind getting down on your knees.

The best place to pray is at home and the best time is early in the morning when everyone is in bed, and in the evening after everyone has gone to bed. This again requires effort on your part, which God, as I've pointed out, seems to take a particular delight in. Early in my recovery, I meditated and prayed both morning and night. It was a solid hour to an hour and a half in prayer. Every day, talking to God. And listening.

I learned early on that if I could start my day with God and end my day with God, somehow he would take care of the rest. And he did. And he does. Praying and meditation became as much a part of my routine as eating. And infinitely more important.

Usually I meditated in a certain chair, but some nights, when there was a full moon, I sat on the floor near a picture window. And I grew to love meditating and praying during a violent rainstorm. The thunder, the lightning, the crashing rain—I figure it's just God making himself heard. But hearing his presence, being aware of it, is a powerful experience.

And I learned that whereas once I would go outside and scream at God about not talking to me, now the more I quietly listen for God, the more he talks to me. I came to understand that God, in fact, never shuts up. I just wasn't listening. But he talks to me in my morning prayers in thoughts, realizations and readings.

God talks to me in meetings all the time, quite often through the least likely people who'll say the most astonishing things. And anyone who regularly attends meetings knows the miracle of showing up and finding that the night's topic is exactly what they need to hear. It happens to me still. All the time. Now I just expect it.

God also talks to me *through* me. Sometimes I'll write about a fear or a problem, about what's bothering me. I'll write down what I want God to do and what he is doing now. The more I write, the more I realize everything's all right, that God's in control. It's my fear that's out of control. And I always hear God talking through me when I'm speaking to someone I sponsor. I'll say the most incredible things, really filled with wisdom and understanding that are not my own. Sometimes I think about taking notes.

But most often, I hear God through Melissa. When I'm having a bad day, she'll encourage me. When I'm confused, she'll remind me of what's really important. When I'm angry, she'll point me back in the right direction. When I'm upset or down, she'll just hug me. God has been talking through her for years; it took the program for me to listen to her and hear him.

Today, we live in a new home, and I meditate in a room designed to be a library. But I'm the only one who uses it, and I use it only for meditation and prayers. So it's little wonder people who enter our home for the first time say they can feel the most extraordinary sense of peace in the library. Or sometimes, I'll see our boys just sitting in there. Keep in mind, this room has no TV, no stereo, just books and windows and chairs. Even a teenager can feel the peace.

When I talk to God in my morning prayers, I can leave my fears there in that room. I can leave my worries there. I can turn over to him everything I'm concerned about. I can hand him my failures, my shortcomings, my imperfections. I can acknowledge that I'll accomplish very little without his help. Then somewhere in there, the miracle happens. I, who battle fear every day, can leave it there for awhile and go on about my day. In peace.

I am no longer on heart medicine. I no longer battle upset stomachs. We live a life infinitely more extraordinary and wonderful than we could have dreamed of ten years ago. We pray over every meal. We still say the Lord's Prayer together as a family every night. Our boys are popular student-athletes at school. Our life is a miracle. And I know it is because we both try to establish a constant contact with God—in our own prayers—every day.

Do I ever have bad days when I have to call on God again and again and again? Of course.

But let me be clear about this: prayer and meditation have led to miracles in my life. Today, there is nothing I cannot trust God with. I can leave him in charge of my family's health, our financial health, my company's health, everything. And as afraid as I have been sometimes, he has never let me down. Never. In fact, I imagine that when it's time for me to meet God, he's going to look me in the eye and say, "It was never as bad as you thought it was, was it?"

Prayer and meditation will change your life too. Yet so many men would rather battle high blood pressure and stomach ulcers than risk letting God in their lives that it just baffles me. I have learned that a lot of men just don't know how. No one ever showed them. But I will show you.

It's easy to begin. You sit and take in the surroundings around you and slowly close your eyes. Breathe through your nose. Slow down your breathing. Then begin saying sort of a mantra, "God loves me," or "Jesus loves me." Sometimes I just might say "God," or "Jesus." Anyway, say your mantra over and over—slowly—in your mind, keeping your eyes closed. Now here's the hard part: *don't make anything hard.* If your face itches, scratch it. If other thoughts come into your head, that's all right. Just put them aside and keep saying "God" or "Jesus," or something, over and over.

You might drift off, you might not. Do this for about ten minutes, which will seem incredibly long the first few times. Just sitting in front of God is new and uncomfortable. After ten minutes, slowly stop saying your mantra. And then pray. Thank God for your wife, your children, where you live, what you drive, the clothes you wear, the food you eat; thank him for your health, for your friends; thank him for everything that's good and wonderful in your life.

Then talk about your day, what's facing you, what your concerns are. Pray that he will guide your thinking all day, and that if you get confused or troubled, he will give you the right thought or action. Then get on your knees and give him everything you have, everything you own. Give him your marriage, your family, your home, your job, your money, *everything*, and say these words, "I give you everything I have, because everything I have you have given me."

Then, most important of all, finish with, "And I Trust You." It doesn't matter whether you trust him or not; you say you do. He knows you're lying, but he appreciates the effort. Soon you will trust him. Then, if you have some reading, a book of scripture or prayers or daily readings, read a couple of those. Then thank God for the time you've had togther, and get up and go about your business. Your life will be different. It has to be. You've just made conscious contact with God.

At night, after you meditate, you might think about your day. Were you resentful, selfish, dishonest or afraid? Do you owe anyone an apology? Do you need to talk to someone at once? Did you hurt anybody? Then get on your knees, ask God for forgiveness, ask him to show you what you need to correct and trust that he will. Your life will be different. Again, it has to be. That's a spiritual law. No one makes contact with God without changing. That's why so few do it.

Sometimes, after your prayers, try just sitting in his presence. It's very peaceful. Very mystical. And the more you do it, the more you'll want to do it.

One guy I sponsor said, "I never know what to say to God."

I told him of a story I heard about a new priest in a French country town who, on his first day, watched an elderly peasant enter the chapel in the early morning and emerge several hours later. The peasant did this for three or four days in a row when the priest, his curiosity piqued, entered the chapel only to find the peasant just sitting in a pew. The peasant looked up and the priest, feeling like he had invaded the old gentleman's privacy, said, "Excuse me sir, I've seen you come here every day, but you don't pray, you don't read; may I ask what you do in here?"

The old man smiled at the priest. "I just like to sit here. I look at God, he looks at me. It makes us both happy."

Step Eleven is like that. It can make God something extraordinary. Your friend.

STEP TWELVE. **Having had a spiritual awakening as a result of these steps, we tried to carry this message to others, and to practice these principles in all our affairs.**

*I*t's a spiritual truth that the more you recognize miracles in your life, the more miracles happen. It was a miracle Melissa found recovery. It was a miracle she didn't die. It was a miracle she was able to forgive me and herself, and that somehow I began taking my hands off and letting her live her own life. And then the real miracles began unfolding: she worked a program that today can only be described as inspiring and beautiful.

She got tired of her rages, and worked hard to end them. She got tired of her spending, and worked hand to end it. She got tired of being possessive and worked hard to let go. I had nothing to do with any of this. I just got out of the way.

Meanwhile, I had gotten tired of my criticism and control. I had gotten tired of nagging her and finding fault with her. I had gotten tired of making her the butt of jokes at parties. And when I was able to quit, to finally stop, I wondered where my mind had been all those years. Because I could finally see what I was doing to the person who is the light of my life.

And somewhere along the line, with her working her program and me working mine and both of us praying and working with our sponsors and other people, something happened: our relationship healed.

I had never stopped loving her. I just had to learn *how* to love her.

The program helped me with *acceptance*. I learned I could accept people, places, things and situations as the way God wanted them that day. The more I accepted Melissa the way she was, the happier, more loving, more wonderful she became. I can't explain.

I quit trying to change her, and she changed into a person even more beautiful, more delightful, more fun than the woman I married.

Acceptance is a principle I practice in business. If a client is unhappy—in spite of our best efforts—I don't get sick with worry anymore. I accept this is the way things are. And I go out and find new business.

Acceptance has helped us with our teenage sons. In fact, I would recommend not venturing into the teenage years without a healthy dose of acceptance.

Acceptance is the result of a "Spiritual Awakening," because it means that rather than freaking out when something isn't perfect—when Melissa is unhappy, for example—I can accept that's the way she is at that moment. I don't have to change her. In fact, now we have a whole new way to deal with each other if one of us is mad—we hug. She'll hug me if I'm upset; I'll hug her if she's upset. A fight is simply impossible if the other person won't cooperate.

A spiritual awakening also means that for the first time, I'm armed with a self-knowledge I've never had before. Rather than spend time trying to make Melissa perfect, I've come to realize perhaps I'm the one who is not perfect. And I can practice this principle in all my affairs now. Was I resentful or selfish with my business partner today? Do I owe one of my kids an apology for my actions? Do I need to go clear up a misunderstanding with an employee? Have I said something to my wife that was unintentionally hurtful? If the answer is ever yes, I need to get up and make immediate amends.

I've also learned I don't always have to be right. My sponsor once told me he thought I'd rather be right than happy. That was true, I told him, because being right *makes* me happy. I would argue a point to death with Melissa to make her see I was right, and I would only make her mad. I've learned if she wants to do something her way, it's not worth my mental sobriety to worry about it, much less start an argument over it by trying to correct her. Today I'd rather be happy than right. Trust me, being right isn't all it's cracked up to be.

I read somewhere that "if you're not sure whose fault it is, it's probably yours." I've learned I can be wrong and not be killed, that it's okay to admit your defects, that the faster you do it, the faster a relationship can be healed. Today, I simply cannot rest if I think I've hurt Melissa's feelings. The issue for me is no longer a self-justifying "she shouldn't have gotten her feelings hurt," but instead, I think, "How fast can I make amends?"

Love tends to flourish in that kind of setting. As does kindness. "Practice these principles in all our affairs," means that by bringing God into every moment, every situation, every relationship, we are always guided by a spiritual principle rather than a self-serving one. So we are always trying to add to someone's life rather than control it, or manipulate it or run away from it.

Melissa has become the most giving wife and mother. She'll go to the store every day for her boys; she'll go out in the freezing night if one of them says he would like a special kind of ice cream for his sore throat. She has sat through thousands of hours of soccer games in freezing and roasting temperatures. And with the determination of an air traffic controller, she manages schedules so we will all be seated at the kitchen table together for at least one meal a day.

She helps the boys with their homework, types their papers, serves on the PTA board, writes books, shuttles carpools, does her garden club thing. She goes to her recovery meetings every day, and she is an inspiration to countless drug addicted women. Yet when I get home she makes me feel like I'm the most important person in her life.

I can see God operating through Melissa in the way she works with other women, and there have been so many. I've opened the front door and found a quivering, shaking woman standing on the porch holding a syringe. I cheerfully announce, "Honey, it's for you." Women call frequently throughout the day, and Melissa gives each one a part of herself.

Her boys adore her, yet they're blissfully unaware of the impact she has on other drug addicts' lives. I am. And I'm in awe.

She is so extraordinary I wonder what I was looking at ten years ago; what was there to criticize? And that's the miracle of the program: new eyesight.

"...we tried to carry this message to others..." refers to what is commonly called Twelfth Step work, or working with others. Why does working with others help your marriage? Again, this is a spiritual program, and we're taught in order to keep something you have to give it away. It's odd how taking time from your own relationship to give another man spiritual comfort regarding his relationship is beneficial to you, but it is. As I've said before, it's a very odd program.

But also, the statement that we "try to carry this message to others," is something Melissa and I do with each other. And not a day passes that we don't share some wisdom or spiritual truth from the program. It could be acceptance, it could be saying God's in charge, it could be the issue of forgiveness—but whatever it is, we help each other with it. Daily.

A marriage built on spirituality is an extraordinary relationship indeed. And that's what is different about ours. It's not built on drinking, or drugs, or golf, or work, or kids, or money, or fashion. The fact is, it took Twelve Steps. But we finally found God.

In each other.